**RICHARD A. JENSEN**

# TOUCHED BY THE SPIRIT

*One Man's Struggle to*
*Understand His Experience*
*of the Holy Spirit*

AUGSBURG PUBLISHING HOUSE
MINNEAPOLIS, MINNESOTA

# CONTENTS

*Introduction* ........................................... 5

1. Feathers and All ................................. 8

2. For the Common Good .......................... 15

3. One Lord, One Faith, One Baptism .... ........ 31

4. Seasons of the Spirit ........................... 54

5. A Biblical Understanding of Spiritual Gifts ...... 60

6. The Kingdom Within ........................... 87

7. Pentecostal Theology: Evidence of the Spirit ..... 105

8. We Walk by Faith, Not by Sight ............... 129

9. The Gifts of the Spirit and the Cross of Christ .... 142

10. Feathers Revisited .............................. 153

# INTRODUCTION

The Holy Spirit has moved among us. Pentecost still happens. Some have called this the "Latter Rain." Others have called it the "Charismatic Movement." Still others refer to it as part of a "Third American Awakening." "I've been baptized in the Spirit. Praise the Lord."

These have been some of the religious sounds of the '60s and '70s in America. A growing number of people have felt "touched by the Spirit." The experience most common to this Spirit movement has been *glossolalia,* speaking in tongues. Over the past fifteen years this experience, which was central to the development of the Pentecostal churches, has occurred with increasing regularity in Presbyterian, Lutheran, Episcopal, Roman Catholic and many other churches.

Experience is an important part of the life of each Christian. The gospel of our Lord Jesus Christ speaks to the experiential as well as to the intellectual part of our being. There is nothing wrong with having a "Christian

5

experience." Some of the critiques that I have read concerning this new Pentecostalism have criticized it just because it is an experience. Such criticisms in and of themselves miss the mark. There is nothing wrong with having an experience of the Spirit! Experience is an essential ingredient of Christian life. Experience is just that: experience. It is not theology. Experience becomes theology, however, the moment one attempts to reflect on it, interpret it, and share it with others. Thus there is in America today a wide variety of "theologies of spiritual experience."

Over the past several years the number of books relating and interpreting experiences of the Spirit has increased annually. The literature floods the market. The viewpoints expressed in this ever-proliferating field touch every imaginable base.

Most of what I read disturbs me. I read with a double concern. As I will set forth on the following pages, I have shared many of the experiences which are being talked and written about. That is my first concern. As a brother in the experience I am interested in how others interpret it.

My second concern arises because I am a theologian. Most of the books I read pose theological problems for one who is interested in preserving a classical interpretation and understanding of spiritual experience. Experience interpreted and shared becomes theology. It is either good theology or bad theology. That is, it either agrees with the classic Christian faith as one understands it on the basis of the Bible and one's own confessional background, or it does not. I find that I cannot agree with the theological interpretation given to speaking in tongues and other experiences in most of the literature I read.

I have, therefore, attempted to reflect on and interpret

my own experiences on a biblical foundation and within the theological framework of my own theological tradition. What you read in the following pages represents the present stage of these reflections.

There is a real burden on my heart as I take up this task. People want to know the meaning of spiritual and religious experience. Available books on the subject present myriad viewpoints and problems. There is no way that I can address all the problems that have arisen, all the viewpoints that have been expressed, all the questions people ask. That task is insurmountable. What I can say and do within the pages of this work is limited. I pray that it is helpful in the midst of its limitations.

Undertaking this task I am mindful of the words Jesus spoke to Nicodemus:

> The wind blows where it wills, and you hear the sound of it, but you do not know whence it comes or whither it goes; so it is with every one who is born of the Spirit (John 3:8).

Isn't "theologizing the Holy Spirit" an attempt to box up the wind so that it cannot blow where it wills? That is an ever-present danger. When it happens, when we grasp the movement of the Spirit in rigid intellectual categories, the Spirit may well become *our* spirit. There is obviously a great difference between our spirit and the Holy Spirit. God's Spirit controls us; we do not control him. This truth limits the scope of what we can say about the Spirit. Everyone who writes on this subject must live and work within this limitation. Acknowledging it, we press on to clarify and understand the work of the Holy Spirit.

RICHARD A. JENSEN

# 1

# Feathers and All

January, 1963. A beautiful day in Addis Ababa, Ethiopia. Every January day is beautiful in Ethiopia. 75 degrees. Sunny skies. We had guests for dinner one Sunday noon. The younger couple was a missionary teacher and his wife, newly arrived from America. The other couple was in Ethiopia under World Brotherhood Exchange. Their assignment was to oversee the building of a chapel, library, and classroom building for Mekane Yesus ("place of Jesus") Seminary.

After dinner we sat in the living room and talked. Before I knew it the man from WBE was making a strong and forceful presentation of a phenomenon he had experienced. It was my first encounter with someone who had personally experienced glossolalia. He had lived in southern California where tongue-speaking first broke into the mainline churches. Father Dennis Bennett's Episcopal congregation in Van Nuys is usually pointed to as the originating source of the Pentecostal experience in non-Pentecostal churches.

(The movement that grew around these experiences was usually referred to as the charismatic movement or the charismatic renewal. I feel that these labels limit the full meaning of the word *charisma*. Charisma is a Greek word which means "gift." All Christians are gifted; all are therefore, charismatic. I would prefer to refer to the movement that has arisen as the neo-Pentecostal movement. The word "Pentecostal" in this definition refers to the fact that many of the experiences which are central to this movement, such as speaking in tongues, are central matters also in classic Pentecostal churches. The prefix *neo,* meaning "new," is used to indicate that what is being described is not the Pentecostal church but Christians in Protestant and Catholic churches who share many experiences in common with their Pentecostal brothers and sisters.)

This was an afternoon and an experience I shall never forget. I was engaged by this warm, "Spirit-filled," businessman-builder who was urging me to take speaking in tongues seriously. I still do not know why I listened to him. The stuff he was talking about was not my bag. I was a theologian. I had finished seminary and a couple years of graduate school. Now I was teaching theology to an intelligent group of Ethiopian students at Mekane Yesus Seminary.

The theology I had learned and the theology I was teaching did not leave much room for non-rational concepts or experiences. Having studied Bultmann and Tillich and Bonhoeffer, I had learned how to restate the Christian faith in rational, down-to-earth, pragmatic language. Theology, in the fifties and sixties, was seeking to speak meaningfully to rational, scientific-minded people. Speaking in tongues is irrational. I should have laughed it off. But I didn't. Don't ask me why. I just didn't. I listened.

And, I asked questions, lots of them. "What's the use of it all?" "What's the purpose?" I remember those two questions particularly well. One answer made some sense. He quoted Romans 8:26. "Likewise the Spirit helps us in our weakness; for we do not know how to pray as we ought, but the Spirit himself intercedes for us with sighs too deep for words." He said speaking in tongues is a new language one can use to pray as he ought. The Spirit does the praying for us that way. Interesting.

The afternoon passed. The guests left and the conversation ceased. But I thought about it. What did it all mean? Why did he tell it all to me? I soon found out that I was not the only one he told. He talked to many of our American Lutherans and shared his experiences with them. Some were curious. Some were furious. All were perplexd.

Some of us decided to have it out. We met with him one evening for further discussion and prayer. We talked and talked. It turned out that one of the others had had the experience of tongues back in the States but had repressed it since. We talked some more. Finally the Californian suggested that we pray together. We would pray for the needs of ourselves and others. After we had finished our prayers we would see what the Spirit might do. If we wished the "gift" we could raise our hands and he would pray for us with the laying on of hands. He instructed us that if someone should speak in tongues the whole group should immediately pray for an interpretation. Tongues without interpretations were meaningless in a group, he said. Sound advice!

We prayed. Our friend who had repressed his tongue now spoke in it, and the Californian interpreted it. I held up my hand. He prayed for me. Some tentative sounds began to well up and trickle out of my mouth. Some others had similar experiences. It was scary. It was fascinating. I realized the next day that I didn't believe any of it. What had I done? What had we done? Fools! I checked out my perceptions with two other men. My feelings were confirmed. They didn't believe it either. We thought, however, that we ought to talk about it some more. We met again that night. Just the three of us and our wives this time. We talked some more. I don't know when I've ever talked so earnestly about something. What else can you do when something so strange and different happens to you?

Talk. Finally we prayed again. It happened again. What had been only the faintest hint of a sound the night before suddenly came bursting out of my being with a gusto that just about swept me and everyone else off our feet. It was all nonsense syllables. Nonsense syllables at an unbelievable rate of speed. The sounds were mostly consonants. My own tongue has not changed much to this day. I have never heard another quite like it. Every tongue is different.

Some people speak in different tongues at different times. Most of these tongues sound like pure nonsense. Others sound like they could be a language. There are those who claim to have recognized a language that was spoken in tongues. I haven't had that experience. If you have not heard anyone speak in tongues you can just imagine it as sounding like a language you've never heard before or gibberish.

After we had finished praying that second night we

talked some more. We still didn't believe it. We met again a third night. Three nights in a row! I had never prayed so much in all my life. What was God trying to do to me anyway? Our friend from California joined us that third night. By then the format of our times of prayer was practically fixed. It has not changed much to this day. We shared insights and talked about concerns and needs that we should pray for. We prayed for them. After the sharing and prayers of praise, petition, and intercession (taking perhaps two hours), we "waited" to let the Spirit speak. There were a few tongues. Each was interpreted, that is, rendered into English by one of the participants who had the gift of interpretation. The interpretations we had at that time were mostly praise of God.

Occasionally an interpretation would be given when no one had spoken in tongues. We studied 1 Corinthians 12–14 to figure out that these were "prophecies." I just about wore out those pages of my Bible that week. In 1 Corinthians 14 Paul speaks about the greater value that the gift of prophecy has over the gift of tongues. Tongues only edifies the one who prays unless it is interpreted. Prophecy (just as interpretation) edifies the whole body. Paul's emphasis is always on what is good for the church. We really could not see any difference in content between what was said after someone spoke in tongues (interpretation) and what someone, led by the Spirit, said without a tongue as introduction (prophecy). We believed, and I still believe, that there is no essential difference between interpretation and prophecy. The only difference is that an interpretation interprets a tongue. A prophecy is uttered without a previously spoken tongue.

Paul's words have proven true in my own experience.

Though tongues were a kind of initial sign that excited us and drew us together for prayer, they soon faded in significance. What became important were the prayers of the group, the fellowship that was built, and the interpretations and prophecies that were addressed to us.

After that third night we finally began to believe that we had been touched by the Spirit in a new and puzzling way. It took a long time to accept that experience. It has taken me even longer to learn how to integrate it meaningfully into the total expression of my Christian life and theology. I had had a strange new experience. It was emotional to be sure, though not emotional in the sense that I had usually thought of. I had heard of Pentecostal "holy rollers" and imagined all kinds of wild excitement and gyrations. This was not our experience. It was emotional in a quietly profound way. It touched us deeply. But we never lost control of ourselves. Some quiet lost and lonely place within me had been "strangely warmed." I would never be the same. I am sure the others involved share my viewpoint about the emotional aspects of this experience.

Three nights we had prayed. We were convinced now. It was real. Now we could spread the word of what had happened to all around us. It's hard to contain an experience like that. You want to share it. You want to tell somebody. Everybody. We did. Some listened. Some came and prayed with us. But the overall effect of our testimony, however, was not a good one. Many people were turned off.

Since then I have read the advice that anyone coming into the experience of speaking in tongues should not tell anyone about it for a year. I wish I had heard or read that then. It is good advice. I did know from reading the Gospels that when Jesus did miraculous deeds among his people he sometimes told them to "tell no one." Other times he told them to spread the word around. Which should it be with glossolalia? I didn't know then and I don't know today. My advice, however, is to tell no one. I have learned over the years that the opportunities for sharing such an experience present themselves. When they do the end results are much better than when I decide who needs to be told. This book violates that basic rule. Somewhere in my heart I feel that the time has come to share my story in this form. What happens to it and with it is out of my hands.

In my initial excitement, however, I didn't keep my mouth shut. How I wish I could take back many of the ill-timed words I spoke! I am reminded of Luther's words concerning one of his ex-colleagues, Karlstadt, who claimed to have moved beyond Luther in his Christian experience. Karlstadt claimed that Luther had only the written Word to rely on, while he was led by the direct guidance of the Holy Spirit. Luther thought that Karlstadt had turned everything upside down. Karlstadt valued the *inner* workings of the Spirit over the *outer* means of the Spirit's presence in Word and Sacrament. As far as Luther was concerned that was the wrong way of emphasizing the Spirit's work. He thought that Karlstadt was guilty of devouring the Holy Spirit "feathers and all" (a reference to the dove as a symbol of the Spirit). Those watching and listening to me in those days must have thought that I, like Karlstadt, had also swallowed the Holy Spirit, *feathers and all.*

# 2

# For the Common Good

*To each is given the manifestation of the Spirit for the common good (1 Cor. 12:7).*

An experience had happened. I had tried sharing it with as many people as I could. That didn't work. Why? What happened? What would work? What was I to *think* about this new-found experience? What was I to *do* about it? As time went by the *thinking* got done in the context of the *doing*.

The doing took place within the context of a prayer group. Some of the people who had shared these initial experiences and some who heard us talk about it got together for prayer. For the next few years this prayer group met on a somewhat regular basis. It was in this fellowship that I learned some of my deepest lessons about the meaning of Christian community.

Probably the most humbling lesson I learned was how community among Christians is created. We didn't do it ourselves! The Spirit called us into community. He did it in a most ridiculous way, or so it seemed. His instrument was the "gift of tongues." The facts are simple. Before this experience took place we of our own will and volition created no community of prayer. We were too weak for that. But the Spirit helped us in our weakness (Rom. 8:26). He helped us in a way we would never have dreamed of. Tongues! Of all things! We were fascinated by this strange new gift/experience. It became the occasion for our meeting together to pray. I am not proud of that. I'm humiliated. Why didn't we get together on our own? Why did we need this unusual "gift of the Spirit" to draw us together? But that's the way it was. That's how the sovereign Spirit chose to create our particular fellowship.

## Shaping a Prayer Gathering

We met together often. It was a Spirit-created communion. But what were we to do in these prayer meetings? How was the gift of tongues to be utilized? As I mentioned earlier, I searched the New Testament, particularly 1 Corinthians 12–14, for an answer. The clearest direction came from 1 Corinthians 14:26-33:

> What then, brethren? When you come together, each one has a hymn, a lesson, a revelation, a tongue, or an interpretation. Let all things be done for edification. If any speak in a tongue, let there be only two or at most three, and each in turn; and let one interpret. But if there is no one to interpret, let each of them keep silence in church and speak to himself and to God. Let two or three prophets speak, and let the others weigh what is said. If a revelation is made to another sitting by, let the first be silent. For you can all prophesy one by one, so that all may learn and all be encouraged; and the spirits of proph-

ets are subject to prophets. For God is not a God
of confusion but of peace.

We followed this advice as closely as we could. We were
interested in doing all things for edification, for the common good.

In our group (attendance averaged about fifteen) only
three or four in attendance had the gift of tongues, interpretation, or prophecy. It has never been and will never be
my contention that any gift of the Spirit, including tongues,
is meant for everyone. Tongues is not, as the Pentecostals
insist, the evidence of the Spirit. (I'll deal more specifically
with Pentecostal understandings in a later chapter.) Passages can be pulled out of 1 Corinthians 12–14 supporting
the Pentecostal view that all should speak in tongues as
a proof of the Spirit's work in the life of a Christian.
1 Corinthians 14:5 is the best example: "Now I want you
all to speak in tongues. . . ." (The missing words of that
verse are ". . . but even more to prophesy.") The non-
Pentecostal view, on the other hand, quotes 1 Corinthians
12:30: "Do all speak with tongues?" The implied answer
to Paul's rhetorical question is clearly, *No*.

In context it seems that this latter passage is the most
important of the two. Paul's whole argument concerning
spiritual gifts is that there are varieties. "To each is given
the manifestation of the Spirit for the common good"
(1 Cor. 12:7). The Spirit ". . . apportions to each one individually as he wills" (1 Cor. 12:11). The body has many
members. Each member is part of the body. Each member
of the body is charismatic. Each has its own gift(s). That
is because each member of the body has been baptized and
made to drink of the one Spirit (1 Cor. 12:13). The one
Spirit enables all people to function in the body of Christ:

the church. Baptism, not tongues, is the sign of the Spirit's work in the life of every Christian!

The argument is sometimes set forth that Paul is only speaking about the function of tongues in public meetings in 1 Corinthians 12–14. The conclusion of this argument is that all Christians should speak in tongues but not all should do so in the public meetings. I remain unconvinced by the hypotheses that all should speak in tongues and that this gift was widespread (universal?) in all of the congregations Paul founded. 1 Corinthians 12 begins as a forthright teaching on the nature of spiritual gifts. "Now concerning spiritual gifts, brethren, I do not want you to be uninformed" (1 Cor. 12:1). I take these chapters, therefore, to be instruction concerning the whole matter of spiritual gifts and not just instruction on how these gifts should be used in public. 1 Corinthians 14 is certainly addressed to the public use of spiritual gifts.

In forming our prayer group and shaping its format we took all of this into account. The format we developed had three component parts. First, reading of Scripture, a hymn or two and a lengthy discussion of our prayer concerns. We shared our needs and burdens. We talked alot about the meaning of prayer and intercession. We were excited by the unexpected answers to prayer. As I look back I'm sure this was a most important part of our fellowship. We were building up each other, building up the church. There was mutual edification aplenty!

Second, prayers of intercession for the needs already detailed were made. Usually everyone prayed. This would take from fifteen to forty-five minutes depending on the size of the group.

Third, time was given over "to the Spirit," as we called

it. This was by far the shortest part of the evening, lasting from five to fifteen minutes. If someone spoke in a tongue we waited for an interpretation. If no interpretation came (which was rare) the prayers were closed. Two or three might speak in a tongue. Each in turn was interpreted "for the common good." Sometimes there was prophecy with no preceding tongue. This happened more and more frequently until that gift which the Spirit had seemed to use to call us together (tongues) was almost non-existent in our group. Tongues, after all, were not what our meetings were about. We met together for the mutual edification of one another. We all brought our own gift(s) to that mutual edification process.

That was our format. All things were done decently and in order. If newcomers were present we explained the whole procedure to them. Normally they knew that they could expect the exercise of the gifts of the Spirit. I don't think such gifts should be used when people do not expect it or when they feel they would be offended by such practice. The common good is the concern, not the chance for someone to display a particular "spiritual gift." The Spirit works to create community, not individual spiritual super-stars!

## The Christian Life: The Vertical Dimension

My own understanding of Christian existence includes a *vertical* and a *horizontal* dimension. The horizontal dimension has to do with our relationship with other people. This is the communal or corporate side of Christian life and faith. The vertical dimension, which is always initiated within the communal context (the church) has to do with our relationship with God. For purposes of discussion and analysis it is possible to isolate our attention on each of these aspects of Christian life. This can be done even though in living that life they are inseparable. Is not our service to our neighbor (horizontal) always a service of God? Does not our life of prayer (vertical) finally focus on our neighbor and his needs? 1 John 5:20: "If any one says, 'I love God,' and hates his brother, he is a liar; for he who does not love his brother whom he has seen, cannot love God whom he has not seen."

The gift of the Spirit called "speaking in tongues" has both a vertical and a horizontal dimension. Paul says that one who speaks in tongues edifies himself (1 Cor. 14:4). I would interpret this to mean that tongues may be used in one's personal devotional life. Tongues may be one aspect of a person's prayer life (the vertical dimension). I don't think that it is out of place to understand Romans 8:26 as a reference to the gift of tongues. "Likewise the Spirit helps us in our weakness; for we do not know how to pray as we ought, but the Spirit himself intercedes for us with signs too deep for words." Tongues is a new prayer language. I hear Paul affirming that in this passage. That's what my friend from California had tried to impress on me as one of the purposes for this gift. It makes sense.

It is important to underscore the vertical character of this gift for the many people who have the gift of tongues but have never experienced interpretation of what they have uttered. Where that is the case, and continues to be the case, the gift of tongues can continue to be exercised by the individual—but only in secret, only in the sanctity of his/her own personal devotional life. That's what Paul says in 1 Corinthians 14. Many church bodies today have given this same advice to their constituency. The gift is to be reserved for use in devotional life. Good advice!

It is consistent with the advice Jesus gave in the Sermon on the Mount. Jesus did not want his disciples to carry out their vertical relationship with God in public. Jesus utters a vehement denunciation to the public display of vertical faith expressions. "Do it in secret," Jesus repeats over and over. "Do it in secret." " . . . your Father who sees in secret will reward you." (Matt. 6:4, 6, 18.)

So it is with the gift of tongues. If it cannot be interpreted for those present, it should be kept in secret. This secretive admonition is often violated. I think it is violated when tongues are used in public with the only apparent intention that they be public. Many neo-Pentecostal prayer groups, particularly when they gather for mass meetings, have times appointed to exercise all "tongues" simultaneously and publicly. I cannot find any biblical justification for such a practice. Isn't this a public exercise of a gift meant for secret times? I think Jesus would be just as upset by this practice as he was by the publicly-pious expressions of some people in his day.

The only time a gift of the Spirit should be used publicly is when it may be for the mutual edification of *all* present. There is no meaningful and ongoing edification for the non-tongue speaker in listening to dozens or thousands of his fellow Christians exercising their "gift." "If any speak in a tongue, let there be only two or at most three, and each in turn; and let one interpret" (1 Cor. 14:27). Any practice which in spirit and tone violates this biblical injunction can only be understood as a means whereby individual Christians get a chance to publicly display their own piety. Public piety is no piety at all. Piety by definition is secret. Only the Father knows the names of piety's bearers. That's his secret. When it ceases to be his secret we cease living by grace alone.

The admonition to secrecy is also violated by neo-Pentecostals when they talk about their gift(s) publicly in a manner that suggests they have something other Christians lack. If you have the gift of tongues keep it a secret, unless perhaps someone asks you about it. Your Father who sees you in secret hears your prayers. Rest in this promise. Don't try to "one-up" someone else by talking and acting as if you have moved up a notch on the spiritual ladder just because you speak in tongues. The temptations to spiritual pride with a gift like tongues seem to be omnipresent. Wouldn't we all like to see ourselves as just a little bit better than our neighbor? After all, what gifts do *you* have? See what *I* have! It really feels good to talk like that. But the minute we talk that way we've lost the heart of what the Spirit's work is all about.

The Spirit's central work is to make Jesus Christ a reality in our life. The Spirit's work is to conform us to the image of Christ. The Spirit's work is to enable us to say, with Paul: "It is no longer I who live, but Christ who lives in me" (Gal. 2:20). If it is no longer I who live then *I* can't boast or brag or be proud of *my* gifts. I have died with Christ. My life is hid with Christ in God (Col. 3:3). When I can trace in detail my spiritual progress then my life is surely not hidden with Christ in God. I know very well what it is. My left hand knows what my right hand is doing (Matt. 6:3). It's not a secret, to me or to God. But, if it's not a secret it may not be of God at all. The gift of tongues is one of the Spirit's many gifts. If you have it, keep it a secret!

## The Christian Life: The Horizontal Dimension

In the vertical dimension of the Christian life, the gift of tongues is a secret. The horizontal dimension of the gift of tongues is not a secret. It is used for the common good, the upbuilding of the body of Christ. The question, of course, is how do I know or decide if my vertical gift should be used horizontally? At the risk of overstating my point I am going to answer that question by saying that the person who has the gift of tongues cannot answer that question alone. The community helps provide the answer. In 1 Corinthians 14:5 Paul says that the one who prophecies (that is, who gives the message in a language understandable to the group) is greater than the one who speaks in tongues unless someone interprets this tongue, that the church may be edified. The tongue-speaker is dependent on someone else for the use of this gift in public. An interpreter is needed. If someone urges on a group that he can interpret his own tongue (which sometimes happens) then the group must weigh what he says (1 Cor. 14:29). The community may decide that what is said by the tongue-speaking-self-interpreter is not in agreement with their understanding of the Bible and the gospel. The point is that there is no way that anyone can simply declare to the fellowship of believers, "These are my gifts. Let me exercise them." We do not tell the body what our gifts are: *The body will tell us what our gifts are.*

There is an old story about a farmer who was plowing his field. He looked up in the sky and saw clouds forming the letters G P C. He interpreted it to mean "Go Preach Christ." He was ready to enter the ministry. His friends, however, doubted his abilities for ministry. They put a different interpretation on the letters G P C. "Go Plow Corn," they told him. "That's probably what the letters mean." The farmer didn't tell the community what his gifts were. They told him!

With reference to the ministry in particular this relates to what has sometimes been referred to as the "inner" and the "outer" call. Anyone may feel an inner call to the ministry. Unless that call, however, is affirmed by a congregation in the form of a call (outer call) no one can function as a pastor. Christians talk about the "priesthood of all believers." Everyone has the right to function as a priest or pastor. It is precisely because everyone has this right that the priests must select one from their midst to be their priest. Such an outer call prevents spiritual anarchy. We cannot have everyone in the congregation trying to be the pastor! In most churches no one has the right to function as pastor unless he is called for that task. We do not let someone walk into our church and say, "God has called me to be your pastor." Within the priesthood of believers no one has the right to tell us that. We, the body of Christ, determine what one's gifts are. If we extend a call, then the recipient becomes our pastor. If we don't extend a call, we don't have a pastor. No one becomes our pastor until we send out the call.

It is much the same way with any "spiritual gift." No Christian has the right to impose certain gifts on other Christians. We are the body of Christ and individually members of it (1 Cor. 12:27). Individual members with their individual gifts do not tell the body how they will function in the body. The body decides what its needs are, assesses the available gifts, and tells us how it will use us. The Spirit works through the individual members. The church is not to be seen as an enemy of the Spirit. The church is the Spirit's creation, the Spirit's workshop. The Spirit working through the body assigns us our role. The Spirit working through the body lets us know when our gifts, including the gift of tongues, may be used horizontally in life of the body.

It is true, of course, that throughout the history of the people of God, prophets have had to rise up and chastise the institutional church. The need for a prophetic voice is always with us. Before we lift our voices in prophetic chastisement, however, we should be aware that the prophets were almost always persecuted. They were seldom accepted in their own generation. The wisdom of their words became true only with the passage of time. Taking on the mantle of prophecy, therefore, is a lonely and often unrewarding undertaking. The prophet is almost always rejected and seldom knows at the time which words were spoken wisely or falsely. That is God's secret.

Let's look at this in a slightly different way. The emphasis has been that gifts of the Spirit are given for the common good. We cannot claim to have a gift of the Spirit just for ourselves. If I am given a gift of the Spirit I am given that gift for you. If you are given a gift of the Spirit you are given that gift for me. You have to instruct me in the ways I can best use my gifts for you. I have to instruct you as to how you may best use your gifts for my edification. Gifts do not belong to us. They are not our *possessions* to use as we please. They are *given* to us for the common good. Remembering and practicing this communal understanding of the Spirit's gifts can prevent us from engaging in practices which destroy rather than build up the body.

## Two Dangers

As mentioned before, our prayer group had three aspects. They were the sharing of needs and prayer concerns, intercessory prayer and a time given "to the Spirit." In the early months of our fellowship some of the group members asked to be prayed for with the laying on of hands that they might receive the gift of tongues. It was not long before we saw some real dangers in this practice. One danger was that it focused too much attention on a single gift of the Spirit: tongues. A second danger was the idea that one who had the gift of tongues could pass that gift on to another person through prayer (as if anyone could hold or withhold the gift). We sought, therefore, to erect some safeguards against these practices.

To combat the first danger (isolated attention on the gift of tongues) we tried to emphasize that Christians live in constant openness to the work of the Spirit. Christians are those people who live out their lives in constant expectancy that God will pour his Spirit upon us through his Word, through Baptism and through the Lord's Supper. Christians are always on the way to these signposts of the church, expecting to receive fresh pulses of God's present Spirit. The laying on of hands and prayer for the children of God is a repeatable act by which the Spirit's presence and work is invoked over us. When we do this, however, we do not tell the Spirit what gifts we want. The Spirit gives or apportions to each one *individually as he wills* (1 Cor. 12:11).

The Spirit gives us what is best for the common good, for the church. In our prayer group if someone wished prayer and the laying on of hands for the gifts of the

Spirit we prayed and laid on hands. We did not pray that anyone receive a gift that we named specifically. We prayed for whatever the Spirit chose to give in order that our fellowship be built up and strengthened. We prayed. We laid on hands. We let the Spirit *charismatize* as he saw fit.

A careful reading of the Pauline material in the New Testament reveals that there is a wide variety of charismata which the Spirit gives to his people. The primary charisma given to all God's people is the charisma (gift) of salvation. Paul uses the Greek word *charisma* to describe the gift of salvation in Rom. 5:15-16 and 6:23. Lists of particular charismata appear in 1 Corinthians 12:8-10, 28-29 f.; 13; Romans 12:4-8 and 1 Peter 4:10-11. A study of these lists shows that the Spirit's charismata range from the seemingly unnatural or supernatural gift of tongues to the seemingly natural gift of administration. The body of Christ needs a wide variety of gifts to function properly. *Who gets what* is the task of the Spirit to determine. A Christian thanks God for the charisma of the gospel received in baptism and prays that the Spirit charismatize him for his task in the body as the Spirit sees fit. That's how we prayed for people. The common good, not individual preference, was the focus of our prayers.

The second danger (that one who had the gift of tongues could "pass it on" through the laying on of hands and prayer) was faced in a simple way. It has already been indicated that we sometimes did pray for people with the laying on of hands. *Several* of us would join in that prayer and hand-laying moment. Care was taken that those who prayed at a time like this possessed a variety of charismata. The focus was not on one who had the gift of tongues praying for someone else to receive that gift. The focus was on the prayers of God's community for one of its members that that member might be charismatized by the Spirit in the Spirit's own way. The common good. That was always the goal.

As mentioned before the exercise of the gift of tongues gradually diminished in our corporate fellowship. Very quickly the interpretation of tongues and prophecy became more important than tongues. Interpretation and prophecy edified everyone! These interpretations and prophecies were quite specific at times. The general tenor was praise of God. But there were also words of admonition, instruction, and guidance. "Singing in the Spirit" came with increasing frequency. (See 1 Cor. 14:13 ff.) At first these songs were in tongues. Someone interpreted the meaning. I will never forget someone singing a four line stanza in a tongue and another interpreting that with a four line stanza of poetry! Increasingly the songs came in English. Harmony was added. Two or three sang at the same time totally unaware of what the other(s) was going to sing or say next. Yet it blended into beautiful polyphonic sound. Listening to and singing those songs was a unique experience. I still cannot explain it.

## "I Believe in the Holy Spirit . . ."

"If you can't explain it how can you do it?" "How do you know that all of this comes from the Spirit?" "Couldn't you have been deceived?" I've heard those questions a hundred times. "How do you *know?*" That seems to be the central question. The Pentecostal churches normally claim that they do know. Their claim is that speaking in tongues is *proof* and *evidence* of the Spirit's work. I don't accept this Pentecostal teaching. *I don't know.* I hope no one ever succeeds in getting me to say that I do know. When I speak in a tongue I don't *know* if that is really the Spirit's work. When I interpret another's tongue or prophecy I don't *know* that those words come from the Spirit. When I sing in the Spirit I don't *know* if that is the Spirit singing through me. Let me say it again: "How do you know this is all from the Spirit?" Answer: "I don't." ". . . for our knowledge is imperfect and our prophecy is imperfect . . ." (1 Cor. 13:9).

When I go to church on Sunday morning I confess the same creed everyone else confesses. I say with all God's people, "I *believe* in the Holy Spirit. . . ." *The church has never claimed to know.* It has never claimed that it walks by sight, by proof, by evidence. The church and its members walk *by faith.* We *believe* in God the Father almighty. We *believe* in Jesus Christ his only Son our Lord. We *believe* in the Holy Spirit. That's our confession. That's my confession. That's all I can say about my experience with spiritual gifts. I *believe* that they are the work of the Spirit. To say more than that would be to say more than the church ever said about the work of the Spirit. I belong to the church. I don't have access to new knowledge or new experiences that other Christians don't have. I believe. Someday someone might convince me through Scripture or common sense that all my experiences were deceptions. I don't think that will happen. But it might. For me to say it couldn't happen would be to disinherit the Christian *faith.* I believe. I am part of a community that believes. I will share what I believe with you. You share what you believe with me. Together we will walk *in faith* towards the day when we no longer see in a mirror dimly (1 Cor. 13:8-13).

But let us walk *together* towards that day. I with my gifts, you with yours. I with my experiences, you with yours. And let's build one another up, help one another out as we walk side by side, hand in hand. Let's walk together for the common good. We will all be richer for the walk.

# 3

# One Lord, One Faith, One Baptism

> *There is one body and one Spirit, just as you were called to the one hope that belongs to your call, one Lord, one faith, one baptism, one God and Father of us all, who is above all and through all and in all (Eph. 4:4-6).*

I had had some new experiences with the Spirit. What was I to think about them? I could not just think about these experiences in the context of a small prayer group. I was more than a private person, more than a person who attended a prayer group occasionally. I was also a public person. I was a pastor and a teacher. How could I share the experiences and insights I had with this wider audience? These experiences did have and still have a profound effect on me. The life and work of the Holy Spirit became something quite real and near. I had to rethink my theology in the light of this experience. I had to interpret this experience in the light of my theology.

What could I tell the congregation and the students? I had already learned by experience that I couldn't just tell everybody that they ought to consider speaking in tongues. That wasn't my job. Giving out gifts of the Spirit was the Spirit's business, not mine. What was my job? I determined that I could make people aware of the reality of the work of the Holy Spirit, sensitize them to his work and then let him do as he willed. I re-discovered that it is not uncomfortable for a Lutheran to impress on people the reality and meaning of the Holy Spirit. This works very naturally by emphasizing that the Spirit is that power which is present and happening in the Word and the Sacrament. Preaching should be a living word of God. Baptism and the Lord's Supper could be understood as places of Christ's present activity.

So far so good. Preaching ought to be a place where God's Spirit speaks a word of forgiveness and absolution to all who hear. The Lord's Supper ought to be a place where the Spirit touches us with his healing hand through the instruments of bread and wine.

The problems began with an examination of baptism. Many refer to the gift of tongues as "baptism in the Spirit." If that was true, what was the role of infant baptism? I was told by some and I have read in a number of places that baptism preferably "believers baptism," should be understood as *chapter one* in God's work with us. The second chapter of God's work in us, the *second* baptism, is spiritual experience and particularly the gift of tongues. According to this line of thought, infant baptism is baptism with water; tongues is baptism with the Spirit. Infant baptism is a formal churchly ritual; tongues is a personal experience. Infant baptism is administered by the church and the pastor; tongues is a baptism by the Holy Spirit. Infant baptism is a sign of things to come; tongues is the reality itself. What about this popular viewpoint?

To resolve the question of the relation of infant baptism and the "baptism in the Spirit" I began to read the book of Acts more carefully. I hadn't paid too much attention to Acts in my reflections on glossolalia. In shaping our prayer group we relied heavily on 1 Corinthians 12–14. Acts seems to pose more serious theological problems. The encounter between Peter and the non-Jewish Cornelius in Acts 10–11 is a good example. Cornelius and his fellow Gentiles received the Holy Spirit when Peter preached to them. Peter's friends knew they had received the Spirit. "For they heard them speaking in tongues and extolling God" (Acts 10:46). Tongues was the sign that they had received the Spirit. *Then* they were baptized. Receipt of the Spirit and baptism appear as two different events in this text. What did that do to my understanding of baptism?

Two important questions arise when one attempts to understand the New Testament in relationship to classic Lutheran teaching concerning baptism. 1) Does the New Testament teach one or two baptisms? 2) What is the relationship between infant baptism and the work and gifts of the Spirit?

1) *Does the New Testament teach one or two baptisms?* The New Testament teaches two baptisms. One is John's baptism. One is Jesus' baptism. One is a pre-Christian baptism with water and is a *sign of human repentance*. The other is a baptism with water and the Spirit and is a *sign of God's presence and activity*.

The story of John the Baptist is told with amazing similarity in all four gospels. (See Matt. 3:1-7; Mark 1:1-11;

Luke 3:1-21; John 1:6-8, 19-34). The accounts in Matthew, Mark, and Luke have four elements in common.

a) John the Baptist is understood in the tradition of the Old Testament prophets. In each case portions of Isaiah 40 are quoted as prophetic of John's ministry. John is the voice of one crying in the wilderness, "Prepare the way of the Lord." His clothing (camel's hair, leather girdle) and his eating habits (locusts and wild honey) would have reminded those familiar with Hebrew Scripture of the Old Testament prophet, Elijah (2 Kings 1:8). John the Baptist is understood as an Old Testament-like, pre-Christian figure pointing the way to one who is to come.

b) The message of the "preparer of the way" is a message of *repentance*. He preached a baptism of repentance for the forgiveness of sins. It is important to note who it is that is the active agent in John's baptism. The active agent is the one who repents. Men and women repent, *get themselves ready*, for the coming of the Messiah. Baptism with water in this case is a ritual sign of human preparedness.

c) John knew that this baptism of human preparedness was only a temporary stage in God's work with his people. Someone greater than John was coming. He had a different baptism to offer, a baptism with the Spirit. "I have baptized you with water; but he will baptize you with the Holy Spirit" (Mark 1:8. See also Matt. 3:11 and Luke 3:16). John's baptism was a baptism of human preparedness. The ritual sign was water. Jesus' baptism, however, was to be a baptism of God's presence. God, not man, would be the active agent in the new baptism with the Spirit.

d) John baptized Jesus. Though John protested this action (he thought Jesus should baptize him) Jesus insisted John baptize him in order to fulfill all righteousness. During the baptismal process, however, the scene of action shifted suddenly from an act of man to an act of God. The heavens opened and the Spirit descended on Jesus like a dove. A voice from heaven spoke, "Thou art my beloved Son; with thee I am well pleased" (Mark 1:11. See also Matt. 3:17 and Luke 3:22). Jesus is seen to be the "Son" of God. He is the one filled with the presence of God; God's Spirit rests on him.

In John's gospel we are told clearly that it is because Jesus was anointed with the Spirit's presence that he would baptize with the Spirit. John the Baptist speaks. He says the one who sent him to baptize with water had told him, "He on whom you see the Spirit descend and remain, this is he who baptizes with the Holy Spirit" (John 1:33).

John had baptized with water. That was a baptism of human preparedness for what was to come. Jesus was the one who was to come. He was the presence of God with man. God's Spirit was on him. His baptism, therefore, would not be a baptism of human preparedness. *Baptism in Jesus' name was a baptism in which God acted. It was baptism with the Spirit!*

There are, therefore, two types of baptism taught in the New Testament. The difference between these two baptisms is that one is pre-Christian baptism and one is Christian baptism. It is a mistake to identify John's baptism with water with Christian infant baptism thereby making baptism with the Spirit *a second Christian baptism.* There are *not* two types of Christian baptism taught in the New Testament. To insist on two types violates the meaning of the New Testament witness to baptism. There are two baptisms to be sure. One is *pre*-Christian; the other Christian. Christian baptism is *one* baptism with water *and* the Spirit.

## Baptism with the Spirit

The New Testament phrase "baptism with the Spirit" needs closer investigation. Pentecostals and neo-Pentecostals alike load this phrase with significant meaning. It is used so often in the contemporary discussion and given so much importance that one would expect to find the phrase "baptism (or baptized) with the Spirit" throughout the book of Acts and the rest of the New Testament. This is not the case, however. The term occurs in only two connections throughout the entire New Testament. First, John the Baptist promised that after him would come one who would baptize with water and the Spirit. We have just examined these passages. Secondly, Luke indicates that the promise referred to by John was fulfilled on the day of Pentecost when the disciples were "filled with the Holy Spirit." The only other reference to "baptism with the Spirit" is in Acts 11:16 where Peter interprets the Gentile Pentecost which he experienced with Cornelius by referring to John the Baptist's promise and the experience of the disciples at Pentecost.

It is very difficult, therefore, to maintain that "baptism with the Spirit" was a widespread experience in the early church. It would be much easier, on the basis of the texts, to argue that only the disciples were "baptized with the Spirit," that what happened to them was unique, and that Christians after the Pentecost experience were baptized with water in the name of Jesus for the reception of the Spirit. That is certainly the conclusion of the Pentecost narrative in Acts 2:37-39!

Chapters 1 and 2 of Acts appear to form a single story. In Acts 1:1-5 Jesus tells the disciples to wait in Jerusalem,

". . . for the promise of the Father, which he said, 'you heard from me, for John baptized with water, but before many days you shall be baptized with the Holy Spirit.'" Here we see the use of the phrase, "baptized with the Holy Spirit."

The promise which Jesus spoke of is seen to be *fulfilled* in the Pentecost story in Acts 2:1-13. The disciples were "filled with the Holy Spirit" and began to speak in other tongues as the Spirit gave them utterance. Peter's lengthy Pentecost sermon interprets the event and the meaning of Jesus' life and death for the crowd that had gathered. God raised Jesus from the dead and exalted him at his right hand, said Peter. In this exaltation, ". . . Jesus received from the Father the promise of the Holy Spirit." Having received the Father's promise, Jesus, in turn, pours out this Spirit on the disciples (Acts 2:32-33).

If this were the end of the story we might well assume that we, like the disciples, should receive the "filling" of the Spirit with the sign of speaking in tongues. This is not the end of the story, however. The end of the story and the goal of the whole Pentecost narrative is told in Acts 2:37-39. The crowd wondered what it should do in response to Peter's proclamation of the Christ event. "And Peter said to them, 'Repent, and be baptized every one of you in the name of Jesus Christ for the forgiveness of your sins; and you shall receive the gift of the Holy Spirit. For the promise (note the constant re-occurrence of this word!) is to you and to your children" (Acts 2:38-39).

The Pentecost narrative presents us with a simple yet profound theological choice. With whom are we to identify ourselves in this narrative? Do we identify ourselves with the disciples who were "baptized with the Spirit" or do we identify ourselves with the crowd who were baptized in the name of Jesus" in order to receive the gift of the Holy Spirit? I think the answer to that question is self-evident. We must identify with the crowd.

The disciples occupy a unique position in the Christian story. Our lives and our experiences are not like theirs. We were not in the Upper Room when Jesus breathed on them and gave them the Spirit. We were not with them on Pentecost day when they were "baptized with the Spirit." We belong with the crowd and with all of the others throughout the New Testament narrative who were *not* baptized with the Spirit!! Like them we are baptized in the name of Jesus and thus receive the gift of the Holy Spirit. The term "baptism with the Holy Spirit" cannot bear the load of meaning that Pentecostals and neo-Pentecostals assign to it. The New Testament evidence is simply not there. It is dangerous to use a biblical phrase like "baptism with the Spirit" to refer to experiences and realities which that phrase was never meant to include.

My point has been to show that the New Testament does not teach two Christian baptisms. Any reference to two baptisms is a reference to a pre-Christian water baptism and to a Christian-water-and-the-Spirit baptism. This can be seen clearly in the narrative in Acts 18 and 19. We discover in this passage that there were early Christian disciples of John who knew only of John's baptism with water. That seems to be the case with Apollos. " . . . he knew only the baptism of John" (Acts 18:25). Priscilla and Aquila, therefore, had to expound the way of God to him more accurately (Acts 18:26). This took place in Ephesus. When Paul came there (Acts 19:1) he found some disciples who had not received the Spirit when they were baptized. They

hadn't even heard of the Holy Spirit! They had been baptized only into John's water baptism. Paul decided that
they needed to be re-baptized. John's baptism, after all,
was a ". . . baptism of repentance telling the people to
believe in the one who was to come, that is, Jesus" (Acts
19:4). Since this is the *only case of re-baptism* in the New
Testament, it is important to understand the story's focus.

Acts 19:1-6 talks clearly about two baptisms. One was
John's baptism. That baptism did *not* include the Holy
Spirit. Paul wished these Ephesian disciples to have the
Spirit. He, therefore, baptized them in the name of the
Lord Jesus. Notice that! Paul baptized them in the name
of the Lord Jesus in order that they might receive the Holy
Spirit. The Ephesian disciples received the Spirit as *passive
recipients* of the act of God through baptism. Part of that
baptismal ceremony was the laying on of hands. After
they were baptized with the laying on of hands in the
name of the Lord Jesus they possessed the Spirit. In this
instance the sign of that possession, the sign of their passive
reception of the Spirit, was evidenced by their ability to
speak in tongues.

There are *two* baptisms in the New Testament but *not
three*. The two are John's pre-Christian water baptism and
Jesus' baptism with water and the Spirit. To insist, as some
people do, on *two Christian baptisms violates the meaning
of the New Testament*. Christians are not baptized twice,
once with water (infant baptism) and once with the Spirit
(tongues, "baptism with the Spirit" etc.). Christian baptism
is baptism with water *and* the Spirit.

But isn't there more that happens to the Christian after
baptism, especially infant baptism? Is baptism the end of

our Christian experience? How can spiritual experiences be understood in the context of infant baptism?

2. *What is the relationship between infant baptism and the ongoing work and gifts of the Spirit?*

This may be the most important question in seeking to give a biblical interpretation of the experience (usually focused on "tongues") of many Christians today. The experience called "second baptism" or "baptism with the Spirit" has thrown the nature and meaning of infant baptism into question. Many are questioning the validity of infant baptism. They simply can't see how a *non-experiential* event such as infant baptism can rank with much importance alongside an *experiential* event like "baptism with the Spirit."

I am going to answer this question, therefore, carefully and at some length. I will speak to the overall question (What is the relationship between infant baptism and the ongoing work and gifts of the Spirit?) by asking three closely related questions. a) Why baptize infants? b) Why emphasize water baptism? c) What happens when an infant is baptized? In the course of answering these questions the answer to our larger question should emerge.

a) Why baptize infants?

Christians who practice infant baptism and Christians who advocate "believer's baptism" have searched the Scriptures for passages to support their respective viewpoints. Both sides can support an argument for their position from the evidence. One thing should be clear. No passage in the New Testament *explicitly* states that infants were baptized. Some passages seem to *imply* such a practice. In Acts 16:15 and 16:33 we read that households and families were baptized. Household baptism would seem to imply that infants were baptized. However, the texts do not say explicitly whether they were or were not included.

It should not be surprising that infant baptism is not in evidence in the New Testament. The New Testament period was a time of *mission,* a time when the gospel was proclaimed to adults. The issue of *second generation* Christians (the children of baptized believers) had not yet arisen. The best available evidence indicates that when that question did arise, the second generation infants were baptized. It is the nearly unanimous witness of church history that infant baptism was the normal practice of the early church. The witness of the church's history is a witness for infant baptism. That is one reason why Luther and most of the Reformers decided to retain the practice. The Anabaptists, the first to advocate believer's baptism, broke with fifteen centuries of church tradition.

The most important reason why most churches retain the practice of infant baptism, however, is because it is a practice in harmony with the meaning of the gospel. Infant baptism is an ever present sign among us that salvation is God's act for us. Infant baptism totally captures the offense and scandal of the gospel. It bears a living testimony to the fact that we are Christians because of what God does for us. God alone makes us his children. He makes us his children at a point in our lives when we have done absolutely nothing to be his children. That is the meaning of the gospel. God seeks us. We don't seek God. God makes us his children. We don't become God's children by acts and deeds of our own. "While we were yet helpless, at the right time Christ died for the ungodly" (Rom. 5:6). While we were yet helpless babes in arms, God called us by his name. The gospel message proclaims that God saves the helpless. God saves sinners. Infant baptism is an on-going symbol in our midst that the motion of salvation is a motion *from* God, *towards* helpless man, even helpless babies.

God initiates salvation. He makes the first move. Faith occurs within the arena of that first move. Advocates of believer's baptism understand baptism as a sign of man's faith. It is a sign of human response. But response to what? An advocate of believer's baptism would say that we should be baptized as a sign that we have responded to God's first move (grace). Faith, in other words, is the result of God's initial act. That is precisely what those who accept infant baptism wish to proclaim visibly and concretely. God makes the first move. But, what could testify to the reality of that fact more clearly than the fact that we baptize infants?

But what about faith? Can a baby have faith? That does not seem possible. How can proponents of infant baptism reconcile their position with the clear statement of Mark 16:16: "He who believes and is baptized will be saved?" Doesn't that mean that believing comes *before* baptism? An infant cannot believe. How can he be baptized? That puts the question quite simply. It is not that simple, however.

A careful study of the New Testament indicates that faith is most often understood to be God's creation. Faith is not man's response to God's first move towards him. Faith is what happens to us when God grasps us with his love and grace. Infant baptism is one of the visible and public instances of God reaching out to us. It is out of the crucible of that reaching out of God to man that faith is created. *Faith happens when God grasps me.* That's why we baptize infants! Where faith is understood as man's grasping for God, only adults are baptized.

One of the biblical pictures used to describe God's act for man is the picture of *adoption*. Suppose you are going to adopt a child. That child may not know that you even exist. Infant children seldom know their adoptive parents exist. When the judge speaks the legal word, however, and the legal papers are signed, that *unknowing child becomes your child*. An event happens quite apart from the child. The moment it happens he becomes your child. His whole status in life is changed. He now has new parents. (Can you see the parallels between the adoptive process and the infant baptismal process?)

The adopted child is your child. That is true whether he knows about it or believes it to be true. As your child grows he may *accept* his status as your child. That's what faith is like. *Faith accepts a new status*. The child's acceptance of his status as your son or daughter is not what makes him your son or daughter. He is your son or daughter because of an event that occurred. Likewise *our faith does not make us the sons and daughters of God*. We are God's children because of an event (baptism) that has happened to us. We may accept that status: faith. Or, we may reject it: unbelief.

This illustration helps to clarify the role of faith. It is not our faith that makes us God's children. We are God's children because God calls and names us his children. Faith does not create our status as the children of God. Faith accepts its new status. Unbelief, on the other hand, rejects what God offers.

Let's carry this analogy one step further. How would we

as adoptive parents treat a disobedient child? Does a child's disobedience disqualify him from being our child? Normally it does not. His disobedience, however, does put a strain on our relationship. As parents we seek to get that relationship straightened out. Sometimes we have to discipline the child to renew the relationship. Other times we reach out to him in love. Parental love is long-suffering.

Apply this analogy to our relationship to God. God has made us his children. He has adopted us as his own. What happens when we disobey him? Does God immediately kick us out of his family? Does he tell us that we must mend all our ways and our doings before we can be his children again? Certainly not! By our sins we put a strain on our relationship with God, but he does not simply respond by threatening to kick us out of his family. He seeks to restore the broken relationship. He may discipline us. He may reach out to us again and again with his love and forgiveness.

Once God has called us his children (infant baptism) he does not let us go easily. His mercy and grace pursue us down the ever winding pathways of our lives until he holds us firmly in his grasp. What a fantastic God! He doesn't want to let us get away. His love just keeps reaching out for us. He reached clear out to the cross. He offered and continues to offer his love that he might catch and hold us firmly as his children. Our baptism is a pledge God makes to us. He doesn't want us to get away from him. He has called us his own and he pledges us his allegiance. He'll come and get us when we fall. That's the pledge God makes to us in the event of baptism!

b) Why emphasize water baptism?

The issue that generally lies behind this question is the

two baptismal theory of a water baptism and a Spirit baptism. Shouldn't our emphasis be on Spirit baptism? We already indicated that the two baptisms in the New Testament are not water baptism and Spirit baptism. The two baptisms in the New Testament are John's pre-Christian water baptism and Christian baptism with water *and* the Spirit. Christian baptism with water *is* baptism with the Spirit. Water and Spirit cannot be separated! The Spirit uses the water. Water, therefore, should be understood as a visible extension of the incarnation. God came to us in the flesh and blood of Jesus. He continues to come to us in the material stuff of water. Materiality is God's way of coming to us. "Material" is not the opposite of "spiritual." Quite the contrary. God uses the material world as a vehicle for his spiritual, life-giving presence.

Water is a particularly appropriate sign for baptism. In our daily life in this world we cannot have *life* without water. We can't be *clean* without water. Water is an absolutely indispensable ingredient for life and cleanliness. That's what baptism is about. It gives life. It cleanses us from sin. Water is a very fitting baptismal symbol!

How much water should be used? Believer's baptism is accomplished through immersion. Is immersion a better way to baptize than sprinkling? Is immersion more faithful to the New Testament evidence concerning baptism? The answer to both questions is probably yes. Luther thought that baptism should be done by immersion. According to Romans 6, to be baptized is to be *buried* with Christ. Immersion would capture the meaning of the baptismal event much better than sprinkling. Immersion would also be a better representation of water's function in giving life and cleanness. Churches practicing infant baptism might find more meaningful ways of highlighting the use of water in the baptismal service.

The difference between infant baptism and believer's baptism, however, is not a matter of how much water should be used. The difference is not between immersion and sprinkling. Infant baptism could be done by immersion. The differences arise around the questions: 1) who should be baptized, and 2) who is the active agent in baptism?

Who should be baptized? We've already answered that question: infants. The reason infants are baptized is the answer to the second question, who is the active agent in baptism? Baptism is an event in which God acts. Romans 6 makes that quite clear. The context of that passage is Paul's attempt to answer the question about the relation of sin and grace. Paul accentuates the role of God's grace. Someone apparently asked him if people should continue to sin just to see how much grace and forgiveness God really has. Paul answers that it is *impossible* for a Christian to keep sinning in such a manner. Why? Because he has been baptized into Christ's death. He has been buried with Christ. He has been raised with Christ to a new kind of life. Baptism according to Paul is an action of God that joins us with Christ's death and resurrection. God gives us Christ's new life. If that is so, we cannot just keep on sinning so that grace may abound. There is new life at work within the life of the baptized.

God does something to us in baptism. God is the active agent in baptism. That's why we baptize infants. God's grace includes helpless babes! God's grace includes all helpless people. When God's Word is joined with this water it becomes a life-giving water. God is a God who gives life to the helpless.

c) What happens when an infant is baptized?

Infant baptism means something about our past, our present, and our future. First, infant baptism means something about our *past*. On our baptismal day we were adopted by God as his children. God called us by name. He claimed us for his family. He joined us with Christ's death and resurrection and gave us new life. Secondly, salvation became a *present* reality in our lives through our baptismal event. The Holy Spirit makes the grace of Christ happen in our lives today through visible things like water. The Spirit gave us salvation in our baptism.

The fact that salvation has been given to us, is a real comfort. It reminds us that being a Christian is a result of something God does for us, not something we do for God. We don't always *feel* like Christians. We don't always *look* like Christians. Sometimes we just don't *see* the fruits of Christian living we would like to see. There are times when we wonder if we are Christians at all. At those times we should remember that we have been baptized. Our Christianity does not ultimately depend on what we see and feel in our selves. We are Christians not because of what we see and feel but because of what we have *heard*. "Faith comes from what is heard" (Rom. 10:17). In baptism we have *heard* God call us by name. We have heard his Word. He called us his own. He means what he says.

The next time you doubt your status as God's child say to yourself, "I am baptized." That is not a magic formula, but a reminder that God has called you his own and has pledged to go with you throughout your life holding you in the hollow of his hand. You might doubt your own "Christianness." You cannot doubt God's promises. Being a Christian is to trust God's promises.

Third, infant baptism means something about our *future*. With reference to our baptism Paul says, "For if we have been united with him in a death like his, we shall certainly be united with him in a resurrection like his" (Rom. 6:5). Our baptism is not completed when the pastor says, "Amen." Our baptism is only completed when that which baptism symbolizes (death and resurrection) takes place once and for all on the last day. To be baptized is to be condemned to die. It is dress rehearsal for the last day. Baptism is resurrection practice. We live our lives in the trust that the God who raised us once from the burial waters of baptism will raise us again the next time we get buried. God raised us before; he will raise us again. To live out one's baptism is to live toward the final day in the confidence that we have already rehearsed and practiced death and resurrection. We need not fear what we have already experienced!

It is true that Christians who believe in infant baptism often talk as if baptism were only something that happened "once upon a time." That's unfortunate. The New Testament gives us a much richer and fuller definition of baptism. St. Paul, in particular, understands Christian life to be a life lived under the umbrella of Christian baptism. Baptism embraces the totality of our existence: past, present, and future. Baptism announces who we are. It promises what we shall be. And, so importantly, it calls us to a life of daily repentance.

Luther asks, "What does baptism mean for daily living?" Listen to his answer. "It means that our sinful self, with all its evil deeds and desires, should be drowned through daily repentance; and that day after day a new self should arise to live with God in righteousness and purity forever." Baptism means something about day by day Christian life. It is related to our *ongoing experience* as God's children. Baptism and experience are not opposed to one another. Baptism without ongoing, continual experience is not sufficient for salvation!

The daily baptismal experience has many names. It may be called *repentance*. Unfortunately, repentance is often understood as an "I can" experience. "I am sorry for my sin. I *can* do better. I *can* please you, God." So often we interpret repentance as our way of turning to God. That cannot be. Christianity is not about an individual turning to God. Christianity is about God turning to us.

In repenting, therefore, we ask the God who has turned towards us, buried us in baptism and raised us to new life, to continue his work of putting us to death. Repentance is an "I can't" experience. To repent is to volunteer for death. Repentance asks that the "death of self" which God began to work in us in baptism continue this day. The repentant person comes before God saying, *"I can't* do it by myself, God. Kill me and give me new life. You buried me in baptism. Bury me again today. Raise me to a new life." That is the language of repentance. Repentance is a daily experience that renews our baptism.

*Conversion* is another daily baptismal experience. Conversion could be defined as the daily practice of baptism, a daily death to self. Some Christians make the same mistake in interpreting conversion that others make in interpreting infant baptism. That is, they understand conversion as a *once for all* event in the past. A particular day or occasion is pointed to as the time of conversion. Their conversion experience is said to mark the beginning of their Christian life. They are converted once. From then on they become responsible for their life before God.

Conversion, however, is not a once-for-all, past tense event. Conversion happens daily. Conversion is renewal of what God began in our baptism. He turned to us that we might be his. Daily we turn to him acknowledging that he first turned to us. Daily we convert by asking God to continue what he has begun. It is certainly true that on particular days of our life our experience of conversion is strong and vivid. Certain times and experiences stand out above others. But there is no experience of conversion we can have that means that we don't have to turn to God for help again the next day. We never get beyond our conversion experience. Daily we convert. Daily we turn to God asking that he keep his promise.

Repentance and conversion, therefore, can be understood as *daily experiences of baptism*. Finally we can begin to answer the second main question that we have raised with reference to baptism: "What is the relationship between infant baptism and the work of the Spirit?" The Holy Spirit is the life-giving breath of baptism. Through our baptism the Spirit *gives* us life (past tense), *promises* us eternal life (future tense), and *creates* new life daily (present tense). Daily we turn to the promise of our baptism. God promised there that he would give us life, eternal life. This daily turning to God can be called repentance, conversion, and many other things. The point is that Christians rely on God each day to keep his life-giving promises.

God keeps his promises. The Spirit continues to work with us. Daily the Spirit renews and effects the promises made to us in baptism. Infant baptism, therefore, should not be understood in such a way that the work of the Spirit is *confined* to our past life and experience. Infant baptism should be understood as the *liberation* of the Spirit to work in each of us every day. In baptism we receive the Holy Spirit as the earnest, the guarantee, the first fruits, the down payment of his further work in our lives. Paul often compares the work of the Spirit to *earnest* money. When earnest money is paid it is a pledge that *more* will follow. The Spirit's work with us in and through Word and sacrament has this *earnest* character. See 2 Corinthians 1:22, 5:5; Ephesians 1:14.

Infant baptism is, in this sense, our initiation into a charismatic life. The Spirit is *freed* to work in us, to "charismatize" us, as he wills. The biblical injunction to "earnestly desire the spiritual gifts" (1 Cor. 14:1) can, therefore, be understood as a call to daily renewal of our baptism.

How the Spirit carries out his ongoing "charismatizing" work within each of us is his business. He knows what he is doing as he daily works with our lives in bringing us to God's last day. Some days we think we can see clearly what his work in our lives looks like. Some days our experiences of the Spirit's presence are vivid and meaningful. Other days we simply blindly believe, in spite of our experiences, that the Spirit is completing what he started with us.

The Christian life is full of experiences. Baptism is not the *end* of our Christian experience; it is the *beginning*. Daily we are experiencing the Spirit's recreating work within us. Note: *daily* we experience. That daily experience is an experience of faith. We *believe* and *trust* that the Spirit is at work in us, finishing the work he started in baptism. Some of those daily experiences seem to us to be of greater significance than others. But *we don't really know* what is important and significant to the Spirit. We should be careful, therefore, about labelling those experiences. Some, for example, receive the Spirit's gift of tongues. Some are so overcome with that particular experience that they rank it on a par with their baptism. They call it a "second baptism."

Christians do experience "second baptisms." Those who daily repent daily re-experience the meaning of their baptism. *Every day we experience "second baptism."* Every day the God who claimed us in baptism claims us again. Every day the Spirit seeks to work his way and will in us. But it is *his* way and will. We don't know what that should be. There is no blueprint or pattern for it. The Spirit works for you. What he does in and for you is not what he must do in and for me. That is why we must be careful about labelling our spiritual experiences. We simply don't know what the Spirit needs to work in us. Daily we place our lives in his hand. Daily we trust that he will continue to conform us to the image of Christ. We *believe* that he will. We don't *know* how he does it. The Spirit's sanctifying work is *alien* to our being. We don't know therefore that the experience of tongues is more important in the Spirit's work with us than an experience of deep pain and agony. We don't know if the Spirit wishes to work in us through great moments of spiritual ecstasy or through long seasons of gradual growth. Probably both! We don't know. We simply believe that God knows what he is doing with us. God knows how to complete in us what he began in our baptism. What he is doing with us will be revealed to us in eternity. In the meantime the true nature of our Christian growth (death of self) is a secret known only to God.

"For you have died, and your life is hid with Christ in God. When Christ who is our life appears, then you will also appear with him in glory" (Col. 3:3-4).

# 4

# Seasons of the Spirit

*For everything there is a season . . . a time to keep
silence, and a time to speak (Eccles. 3:1, 7).*

After I had experienced some of the gifts of the Spirit
in Ethiopia, I sought to work out what those gifts meant
in terms of the body of Christ. There came a time, in
Ethiopia, when I was somewhat comfortable with my experiences, my interpretation of those experiences, and my
public proclamation of the work of the Holy Spirit as the
energizing power behind all Christian experience.

My comfort was broken when I received a call to leave
Ethiopia and return to the United States in 1965. The call
was to a small Midwestern church college. I was to be
Campus Pastor and a professor in the Religion Depart-
ment. What I had thought through carefully in Ethiopia
was challenged by a new context. How should I treat the
whole subject of spiritual gifts and my personal involvement in them? Should I discuss them publicly? Should I
try to convince others of the validity of such experiences?

I had heard that the attitude toward spiritual gifts was not as friendly in America as it had been in Ethiopia. What to do now?

I decided to keep silent about my experiences. The Spirit was sovereign over his gifts. If he wished me to speak, he could provide the opportunities. In my preaching and teaching I emphasized that the Spirit made the Word (oral and written) and sacraments come to life. The Spirit breathed life on us through Word and sacrament. I bore firm testimony to the life-giving power and work of the Spirit. I did not, however, share in a public way some of the ways that the Spirit had been at work in my life.

Those years are now behind me. Did I do the right thing? Was I afraid of the consequences of what my own testimony might bring? That is certainly a possibility. The mid-60s was a time for rational approaches to theology in academic circles. I obviously did not wish to be branded as anti-rational; that was considered academically irresponsible. In the perspective of time, however, I believe I did the right thing. I have learned some meaningful lessons about the "seasons of the Spirit."

Let me cite one example. Two Lutheran pastors nearby learned that I had been involved with charismatic experiences. First one, then the other, invited me to come and talk to their adult Bible classes. In the first instance the pastor had led his class through an extensive two year course of Bible study. He had then led them through a further study of the book of Acts and the meaning of the Holy Spirit. A young girl from his congregation, enrolled in an Eastern college, had written to him that she had received the gift of tongues. Members of the adult class were curious about the meaning of this girl's experience. Would I come and talk to them about my experiences? I had not sought the invitation. Maybe that was the prompting of the Spirit. He had called me through the church to speak. I went.

As a result of my visit and subsequent visits with the pastor that congregation became heavily and, I think, healthfully involved in the charismatic movement. The pastor is often invited, sometimes by his Bishop, to speak to other groups and congregations in which interest or problems have arisen. Several good things have happened as a result of my affirmative response to that invitation. That's what I mean by "seasons of the Spirit."

In the five years I was at the college I spoke of my neo-Pentecostal involvement only twice in public. I was not involved in any prayer group as I had been in Ethiopia, a fellowship I missed deeply. Such a group would have been helpful.

However, I was surrounded by the fellowship of the congregation to which I belonged. It was good to be reminded that *the local congregation,* in the midst of its ordinariness and seeming weakness, *is our primary source of fellowship and strength.* Neo-Pentecostals can become disenchanted with their local congregation and ministry. The temptation is to move beyond its boundaries to find meaningful spiritual experiences. Any prayer group has the potential for divisiveness and exclusiveness within a congregation. That danger is even greater in a prayer group composed of people from various congregations and denominations that focuses its attention on gifts of the Spirit. Such a group may create its own understandings of what the church should be. It may easily forget that the local congregation is our concrete touchpoint with the Body of Christ and *all* of its members (see 1 Cor. 12!).

Two public speaking engagements in five years. That was just about the extent of my neo-Pentecostal involvement at that time. That was not necessarily my timetable. I *believe* it might have been the Spirit's timetable for me. The Spirit did use those times. That he did so was out of my hands. I cannot take credit for it.

There is a growing belief in me that this is how the Spirit works. He sets up his own timetable. He is indeed sovereign over his gifts, giving to each one individually as he wills (1 Cor. 12:11). He has his own seasons of blessing. We should be sensitive to the Spirit's sense of timing. He won't always work as we want him to. But in his season far more is accomplished than in any time schedule we might work out.

This lesson is not only applicable to spiritual gifts. It applies to all who are concerned with the proclamation of the gospel. We devise our strategies of conversion. We formulate grand evangelism programs. We set careful congregational goals. We pick out an individual to work on for the Lord. These things are important. We should not dispense with them. They must not, however, stand in the way of the Spirit's seasons. "The wind blows where it wills" (John 3:8). Our own plans and goals should never block the wind. That often requires patience. How often it looks as if nothing is happening in our congregation, through our own witness and throughout our own denomination. That's how it looks to us. How does it look to God and the working Spirit? That we don't know. We carry on *believing* that the wind will blow in due season.

After five years as a college chaplain and religion professor I returned to graduate school. For the most part I continued to keep silent about my own experiences. The

Spirit would have to provide opportunities for speaking. I would wait for his season.

My graduate work came to its completion. Through a strange set of circumstances an opportunity to teach at a seminary came my way. There was at that time a renewed public discussion of the neo-Pentecostal phenomena. My season of silence appeared to be over. The responsibility for participating in the public discussion presented itself. I taught a course in which the neo-Pentecostal movement was discussed within the framework of Lutheran theology. A paper I worked out for that course dealing with pastoral guidelines in neo-Pentecostal situations began to get widespread circulation. It was included in a set of documents recommended for pastoral usage throughout the church. Invitations from pastoral conferences to speak on the neo-Pentecostal movement began to come. Plans for this book were made in consultation with the publisher.

The church at many levels indicated to me that the time for speaking publicly had come. The *church told me* when the season for speaking had arrived. I did not tell Christ's body when I was ready. It told me. I am convinced, however, that those public opportunities would never have presented themselves to me had I not observed strict seasons of silence. I take it as another episode in my own growing understanding of the "seasons of the Spirit."

Most Christians are serious about discerning and doing the will of God in their lives. We don't always know, however, what that will of God is for us. There are seasons of our life that appear to accomplish little of what we think to be important. Other seasons abound with fruits of the Spirit that we endorse. In God's timetable we don't really know which of these seasons is the more important. We don't need to know. I am not even sure if we are meant to know. We trust our lives into the hands of the Triune God daily. We believe that he knows what he is doing in and through us. In this process God leads us through different seasons. I have described a silent season and a speaking season in my own life. I don't know what kind of seasons God has in store for you. Be patient. God does his work in you at all times and the results of that work will appear in his own time and season.

# 5

# A Biblical Understanding of Spiritual Gifts

In the Spirit's season I have felt called by the church to speak publicly concerning my own experiences within the framework of the neo-Pentecostal movement. As a teacher called by the church I have found myself facing the challenge of thinking through my own experiences in the light of the Scripture and in contrast to the interpretations given to similar experiences by others.

My procedure in this chapter will be as follows. First, I will state a biblical foundation for understanding spiritual gifts. In the two chapters that follow I will present alternate foundations for interpreting and understanding gifts of the Spirit. Those alternate foundations will be critiqued in the light of the biblical foundations presented here.

This procedure will break the autobiographical flow of my story. Somewhere in this story, however, I must set forth in a straight-forward manner the results of some carefully done theological thinking. Our experiences, my experiences, must be interpreted. They must be thought through in order that experience does not overwhelm and destroy the basic character of the gospel of Jesus Christ which we cherish. I invite you, therefore, to enter with me for some moments into a teacher's workshop.

BIBLICAL FOUNDATIONS
1. *Salvation is by grace alone.*
   For by grace you have been saved through faith; and this is not your own doing, it is the gift of God (Eph. 2:8).

Salvation is a word the Bible uses to picture what it is that God has done for the human race. The Greek word for salvation translated literally means *health*. God has acted in Jesus Christ to grant health to people living in sickness (sin). God gives health to us out of no merit on our part. We have not deserved it. It is God's graceful gift. It comes with no strings attached. It's free. Unconditioned. That's grace! Salvation, health, new life are given to us in spite of our sinful condition.

Grace *alone*. We are saved by God's grace . . . period! Not grace *plus* our response. Not grace *plus* our good works. Not grace *plus* our experience. Grace alone. Nothing can be added to grace. When we add to grace it is no longer grace.

The drive for *more* is the greatest threat to grace *alone*. If there is more, any *more,* then grace is not alone. More is Satan's favorite word. That's what he promised Eve in the Garden of Eden. "You will not die . . . you will be like God . . ." (Gen. 3:4-5). That is very much like what Satan promised Jesus when he tempted him in the wilderness. "All these [the kingdoms of the world] I will give you, if you will fall down and worship me" (Matt. 4:9).

There's *more,* Eve. There's *more,* Jesus. There's *more* for us too! Satan's greatest victory is to persuade us that there is *more*. Then he has succeeded in making a mockery of the gospel. He has made us search for *more* rather than trusting in God alone.

To live by grace alone means to live with the *scandal,* the offensive character of the gospel. " . . . we preach Christ crucified, a *stumbling block* (Greek: *skandalon*) to the Jews and folly to Gentiles" (1 Cor. 1:23). The scandal of the gospel is that there is no room left for *me*. All the religions of the world call upon us to rise up and live for God. Christianity calls us to sit down and die and hear that God has lived for us. Salvation is not our doing. Not one bit of it! It is a gift of God.

By grace alone. Our egos do not like that message. *Self* wants to live, not die. *Self* wants to please God, not be pleased by God. *Self* wants to serve God, not be served by by God. *Self* is offended, scandalized and shocked by the proposition that salvation is by grace alone. If the gospel has not deeply offended our ego/self we probably have not understood the gospel at all. The message of grace *alone* is deeply offensive to the human *I*.

*Application:* A man and his wife spent an evening in our home. She had just been to a meeting geared to charismatic renewal. One speaker in particular had convinced her that she needed *more* in her Christian life. That more was particularly related to spiritual gifts. She was in anguish. She could not be satisfied with the present state of her Christian life. There was a particular *more* that ought to be in her spiritual future. She had prayed specifically for the gift of tongues but had not received it. What should she do? Was there some way in which she was not letting the Spirit give this gift *(more)* to her?

For about two hours my wife and I tried to interpret for her the meaning of grace alone. We pointed out that God's greatest gift or charisma to all people is the gift of salvation. When we say that salvation is by grace alone we mean that it is given to us as an unconditional gift. That giftedness should also mark our understanding of spiritual gifts. A gift is a gift. Any *more* that is to be added to our life by God is also his gift. We cannot, therefore, talk of the gifts of the Spirit in any kind of language that suggests that they will be ours if we only desire them. We can't earn a gift through a sincere desire for more. There is nothing we can do to deserve more from God. There are no formulas, no programs, no list of steps to follow, no blueprint of spiritual exercises that we can perform in order to gain a spiritual gift.

When God gives us salvation through Jesus Christ he gives us everything we need. "For in him the whole fulness of deity dwells bodily, and you have come to fulness of life in him" (Col. 2:9-10). *Nothing can be added to the fulness of God!* God's grace is sufficient. It doesn't need any *more*.

> 2. *The work of the Holy Spirit is to make the grace of Christ happen in our lives today.*
> When the Spirit of truth comes, he will guide you into all the truth . . . He will glorify me, for he will take what is mine and declare it to you (John 16:13-14).

God's love, grace and salvation were at work in Jesus Christ. The Holy Spirit is the name we give to that same work of Jesus Christ as it happens in our lives today. The power and love of God are not only past tense realities. They are present tense realities. The Holy Spirit is the active presence or the present activity of Jesus.

Jesus lived in the first century. We live in the twentieth century. There is a nineteen century gap between us. How is that gap bridged? There are only two possibilities. The first is that it is our responsibility to bridge that gap. We must remember Jesus. We should follow his example. We should be like him in every way we can. In that way we would properly remember Jesus and, by imitating his life, bring him to the remembrance of others.

The second possibility of bridging that nineteen century gap is that it is God's responsibility. That's what the testimony to the work of the Spirit affirms. The God who worked in and through Jesus works in us today. Jesus is not a past tense savior that we are to follow and imitate. Jesus is a present tense savior seeking to transform our lives into his likeness by his powerful grace.

The Holy Spirit is the name we give to the reality that it is God, not man, that bridges the nineteen centuries. The Spirit makes it possible for Jesus to do for us what he did for those men and women of first century Palestine. He healed their diseases; he heals our diseases. He forgave them their sins; he forgives our sins. He restored life to them; he restores life to us. The present tense of these verbs is possible because of the work of the Spirit of God. The Holy Spirit is the present tense, happening-power of God's love and grace in our lives today.

*Application:* The Holy Spirit is at work among us conforming and transforming us into the likeness of the head of the new humanity, Jesus. Often times, however, when we look at our lives, we don't see a whole lot of transforming going on. Many people today are dissatisfied with the spiritual condition of their lives. (Indeed, we might wonder about a person who is satisfied with his life before God!)

I have been asked about this many times. "What is wrong with my spiritual life? Why can't my life look more like that person's life? Why do I seem to grow and change so slowly? Why can't I be more spiritual? My life certainly doesn't look or sound like the lives of the people I read about in so many books on the Spirit. What are my spiritual gifts? I don't speak in tongues or anything. What's the matter with me?"

Such questions are usually questions of comparison. In comparison with the lives of many people around us it often seems that our lives don't measure up. But whoever said that our lives should be like those around us? Our lives are not to be "conformed" to the lives of other Christians. The work of the Holy Spirit is to conform and transform our lives to the life and image of Christ. We don't always know (maybe we never know!) what that means for our own life. We do know that we are to open our lives to the *present activity* and *active presence* of Christ (the Spirit's work) in our lives. But what Christ and the present Spirit does with each one of us is quite different.

The Spirit's present work with each of us is different because we differ from each other. It differs, also, because God chooses to use us in different ways as we function in his body, the church. Some of us receive some *gifts* of the Spirit similar to those mentioned in 1 Corinthians 12. Praise the Lord! All of us receive a measure of the Spirit's *fruits:* love, joy, peace, patience, kindness, goodness, faithfulness, gentleness, self control (Gal. 4:22-23). The greatest gift any of us can receive is the gift of love.

In discussing gifts of the Spirit we must be careful how we distinguish between our responsibility and God's re-

sponsibility. Our responsibility is to pray daily a prayer
something like this: "Come, Holy Spirit. Do the work of
Christ in my life today. Transform me into the image of
your Son."

It is God's responsibility, however, to determine how that
prayer of ours shall be answered. How the Spirit of God
answers that prayer for each of us will be quite different.
We must be careful not to put a straight-jacket on the
Holy Spirit.

The Holy Spirit is at work making Christ happen in our
lives today. He is at work transforming us into the likeness
of Christ. In this transforming work the Spirit is the Lord
of his gifts and fruits. He knows what he is doing. He
knows what we need. We can't set up a list of things
(spiritual gifts, for example) which *we* think all "real"
Christians can or should possess. There is no such list! The
Spirit is sovereign and free as he makes Christ happen in
our lives from day to day. We believe that he is accom-
plishing his work in us too.

3. *God's Spirit is present in outer, visible signs.*
   And the Word became flesh and dwelt among us,
   full of grace and truth (John 1:14).
   That which was from the beginning, which we
   have heard, which we have seen with our eyes,
   which we have looked upon and touched with our
   hands, concerning the word of life . . . we proclaim
   to you (1 John 1:1-3).

The climactic event of salvation history was the enfleshment of God. We call that event the *incarnation*.
God-in-the-flesh. Jesus is God with skin on! God's final
revelation of himself was visible for all to see. This revelation of God is a tangible reminder to us that it is God
who comes to us, not the other way around. We don't

reach God through some kind of internal spiritual exercises. We don't reach God through inner meditation. We don't reach God by making contact with the invisible world within us. We don't reach God . . . period! God reaches for us. That is the meaning of a visible, public incarnation.

The Word (written and spoken) and sacraments (baptism and the Lord's Supper) are *the extensions of the incarnation* in our world today. Where is God at work in our world? Many ask that question. Word and sacrament give public and visible shape to the answer to that question. God always reaches for us. God's reach for us was visible in Jesus. It is visible today in the form of Word and sacrament. The Holy Spirit is the enabling power of Jesus' work in our midst. That means that the Holy Spirit makes Jesus present through the visible, public and outer means of words and water and bread and wine. These material things are the places of God's enfleshment for us today.

The Holy spirit is not an invisible mystery. He does not correspond to the innermost hiddenness of our being. He is not, by nature, within us. The Spirit comes to us from without, from the outside. (That's always how God comes to us.) He is present for us promising to do his work whenever the Word is read or heard. He is present and working in baptism. He is present and working in and through the Lord's Supper. If we want to be touched by the work of the Holy Spirit we know where to go! We read our Bibles. We listen to the word proclaimed. We get together with God's people. We celebrate our baptism. We participate in the Lord's Supper. We expect God's Spirit to work on us, transforming our lives through these visible and outer signs. That's what we expect. Word and sacraments do not automatically guarantee God's presence. His promise, however, is attached to these outer, visible signs.

The sequence of events in the Christian life could be outlined briefly in three words: outer-inner-outer. We have already discussed the first *outer*. The initiating event of every Christian life is the invasion from outside. God comes to us. He comes to us in Jesus. He comes to us in Word and sacraments.

The *inner* result of this outward invasion is that the Holy Spirit brings Christ into the depths of our being. Our *inner* being is renewed and transformed. That is the Spirit's lifetime assignment with our lives. The goal of his work is that, "it is no longer I who live, but Christ who lives in me" (Gal. 2:20).

Outer (God's invasion), inner (transformation into Christ's likeness) and *outer* again. The final outer is that the Spirit leads us through the means of creation (words, water, bread, wine) back to God's creation to perform humble and simple works of love and service for our neighbor. Christian life is finally characterized by the fact that it gives itself away in love to those in need. That's why Martin Luther tried to. empty the monasteries. He understood love of God to mean visible and *outer* acts of charity for God's people, not inner and invisible acts of devotion to God himself.

*Application:* Many people have been upset by the emphasis on spiritual gifts in the neo-Pentecostal movement. Some reject the whole idea. Others live on the edge of guilt because they have not received any of these particular gifts. There are numbers of people earnestly desiring the gift of tongues, for example. For a goodly number that gift does not become a reality in their lives. Serious questions arise. "I've been to many prayer meetings. I've been prayed for with the laying on of hands. I've talked with people who were supposed to be able to help. I've seen the very best, tried the most exclusive prayer groups but nothing works. What shall I do?"

Tucked away in most of these questions is the assumption that the Spirit is possessed by a private prayer group, a special pastor, a hidden interior discipline and so on. Not so! The answer to the question of the presence of the Spirit is not a hidden and private answer. It is a visible and public answer. The Spirit works through the visible signs of Word and sacraments. God's Word, the Bible, is a *public* book. Baptism is a *public* event. The Lord's Supper is a *public* celebration. The Spirit works in these public places. Healthy zeal for the presence of the Spirit in our lives should lead us to these public, outer and visible places of the Spirit's work.

The Spirit "gifts" his people through Word and Sacrament. Gifts of the Spirit are not obtained by special, new, hidden and secretive prayers and supplications. The Spirit works where *all* may hear and receive. Such an emphasis should make it clear that spiritual gifts are in the Spirit's power to give where and when he pleases. To search for spiritual gifts outside the scope of Word and sacrament may easily lead us to replace God's visible promise and presence with our own secretive and private forms of human magic and manipulation.

4. *The work of the Triune God (Father, Son and Spirit) is one life-giving work.*
   In the beginning God created the heavens and the earth. The earth was without form and void, and

> darkness was upon the face of the deep; and the Spirit of God was moving over the face of the waters. And God said, "Let there be light; and there was light" (Gen. 1:1-3).
>
> In the beginning was the Word, and the Word was with God, and the Word was God. He was in the beginning with God (John 1:1-2).
>
> Now there are varieties of gifts, but the same Spirit; and there are varieties of service, but the same Lord; and there are varieties of working, but it is the same God who inspires them all in every one (1 Cor. 12:4-6).

The work of the Triune God is not three works. There is not a work of the Father, a separate and different work for the Son and another separate and distinct work of the Holy Spirit. Father, Son and Spirit do the work of God in different ways. The work of the Triune God is the creation, re-creation and preservation of life. The Father is the origin and source of life. The Father creates life through his Word (the Son). He continually preserves life through the present and ongoing activity of the Holy Spirit.

In the Bible the Spirit is usually associated with the breath or wind of God whereby life is created and sustained. In the story of creation (Gen. 1:2) we read that the Spirit or wind of God moved over the face of the waters. When man was created he received from God the *"breath* of life" (See Gen. 2:7). Man and creation, according to Old Testament texts, are created and upheld by the Spirit (wind or breath) of God. When God takes his breath or Spirit back to himself, man and creation return to dust (Psalm 104:29-30; Job 34:14-15.)

These Old Testament passages serve as an important backdrop for understanding the overlooked Pentecost story in the New Testament. In John's gospel Jesus' giving of the Spirit is told simply in chapter 20, verse 22: ". . . he breathed on them, and said to them, 'Receive the Holy Spirit.'" The work of God, Father and Son, is to give life. In the Bible, to have life is to have the breath (or Spirit) of God. To be given the breath of God, to receive the Spirit, is to have life.

The Bible does not sharply distinguish God's work of creation and his work of salvation as we sometimes do. God has one work: to create and sustain life by his breath. It might be good if in the English language we confessed faith in the Holy Breath rather than the Holy Spirit. That might get the point across. The Holy Breath is God's on-going work of giving life to his creation. That work is always in force.

That is why the Third Article of the Creed is so important. The work of creation (First Article) is past. Salvation (Second Article) is accomplished. The person of the God-head whose work we confess in the Third Article, the Holy Breath/Spirit, is the ongoing present tense work of creation and redemption. He brings the work of creation and redemption to its conclusion on the last day.

God's work of giving life is one work from creation to re-creation (eternal life). We should try to understand both the work of the Son and the work of the Spirit as aspects of the one, all-encompassing work of God. If we separate the work of the Holy Spirit from God's all-embracing work we can only misunderstand the Spirit's work. We shall see some vivid examples of the problems caused by separating the Spirit's work from that of the Father and the Son in subsequent chapters.

5. *Spirit versus flesh refers to the struggle between God and man.*
   The Egyptians are men, and not God; and their horses are flesh, and not Spirit (Isa. 31:3).

The Bible is full of passages which talk about the conflict between flesh and spirit. The way our culture has shaped our thinking we automatically tend to think that this is a reference to a conflict within us. Our spirit or soul fights with our flesh for dominance and control. Once we think like that, we can find many Bible passages which seem to support such a view.

A more careful reading of the Bible, however, reveals that spirit does not necessarily refer to a part of *us*. Spirit refers to God. The struggle presented in Scripture is the struggle of God and his will versus man (flesh) and his will. That spirit and flesh refer to God and man can be seen in the poetic couplet quoted above from the prophet Isaiah. In that couplet it is clear that the words men and flesh refer to the same reality. The words God and spirit refer to a single reality which stands in contrast and opposition to the men-flesh reality.

This understanding of flesh and spirit becomes crucial in seeking to understand a passage like Romans 8 which gives us a classic view of the Spirit's work. The whole chapter tells of the struggle between flesh and spirit. This passage could be read as a story of the struggle between man's higher (spirit) and his lower (flesh) natures. In that case God's Spirit allies himself with our spirit in order to subdue our flesh. With God's help the better part of our nature conquers.

The biggest problem with this interpretation is what it does to our understanding of sin. Sin becomes identified with our lower nature (flesh). Christians become those who have conquered their lower, fleshly nature. Sin affects only a part of us. A part of us is good and a part of us is bad. That is an anemic and unbiblical understanding of sin. In the Bible sin designates the *rebellion of the whole person* against God. Not part of us but all of us is sinful and unclean. We are flesh. We live for ourselves. We are self-centered, and egocentric beings.

The only remedy for selfishness is God. The only conquest of flesh comes from God, from Spirit. Spirit and flesh refer to God and man. The conquest of the Spirit is the conquest of God over our entire life: body, soul, spirit, mind, heart, etc. In Romans 8 this conquest of Spirit over our self is described in at least four ways:

1. The Spirit gives hope to our mortal bodies (vv. 9-11).

2. The Spirit makes us children of God able to call God, *Abba,* "daddy" (vv. 12-17).

3. The Spirit gives us the first fruits of redemption in the midst of suffering. Possessing these first fruits we await, with the whole creation (note that the creation is also to be redeemed!), the final redemption of our *bodies* (vv. 18-25).

4. The Spirit helps us to pray as we ought (vv. 26-27).

Flesh does not refer to a minor problem with the lower part of our being. Flesh denotes the *whole person* whose will is set against God. Spirit denotes the work of God as he breaks our will, turns us around and transforms us into the likeness of his Son.

*Application:* The full importance of a proper understanding of the relation of flesh and spirit in relation to the spirit movement of our time can only be appreciated in relationship to alternate forms of understanding "spirit."

In our next chapter we will take up consideration of an
interpretation of spiritual experiences which identifies
spirit with the best and most interior parts of our human
being. We will make a fuller use of the distinctions we
have made here after we have seen the implications of
understanding human spirit (the good part within us) in
relation to Holy Spirit.

The last three "biblical foundations" which we have discussed have an internal unity. We have talked about God's
order of things as moving from the *outer,* to the *inner* to
the *outer* again. We have also talked about the work of the
Triune God as one life-giving work. We have talked in
this section of Spirit (God) versus flesh (man). These
statements are closely related to each other. God creates, in-
carnates and re-creates life for his people. God is the Spirit
who gives us life. We, as flesh, protest against this gift of
life. We wish to be the maker and builder of our own life
before God. Sin can be described as our "declaration of
independence" from God's gift of life and Spirit. "I can do
it myself," our flesh declares.

The consequence of our declaration of independence is
death. We don't possess life in and of ourselves. The gospel
is God's gracious invitation to accept life once again on
God's terms . . . as a gift. That gift of life is made real
in our existence by the work of the Spirit. When we recognize the priority of God as our Creator and life-giver, God
takes us up into his work and plunges us back into the
arena where he is at work: the creation itself.

This needs to be emphasized in order to avoid the danger
of thinking that the Spirit, and gifts of the Spirit, are meant
to lead us away from the earth to a vaguely defined world
of the spiritual. A working man complained to me about

this one day. Many of his best friends were neo-Pentecostals. They chided him for his lack of spiritual concerns and his poor priority list. He told me, "I've got an ordinary job. Five days a week. Eight hours a day. I do my best and try to serve God in those hours of the week. Some of my friends tell me my job isn't spiritual enough. They've even suggested that I find a different one. Spiritual matters should come first they say. I'm confused. What should I do?"

I have been trying to emphasize that God's life-giving work of creation and redemption does not lead us away from the earth. Redemption is God's way of putting the earth back together again. The unique Christian expression for this is our hope for a *new creation* and a resurrected *body* rather than the ancient Greek hope for the immortality of the soul freed from the body. Redemption does not free us from our bodies or the earth. Christ's redeeming work is to heal our bodies and make our life on earth, here and in the new earth to come, a meaningful life.

In other words, my friend's *ordinary* job was not so ordinary after all. God works in the world he created. He calls us to work alongside him. He calls us to bring *life* to all people. We do that when we tell people the good news of Jesus Christ. We do that when we tend their wounds. We do that when we lighten their load. We do that when we gladden their hearts with a good meal. We do that when we fix their car or repair their shoes or mend their socks or fix their toys. This is our spiritual service to God's world. The ability to do any of these things and countless others is a *spiritual gift*.

St. Paul understood that very well. That's why he told the Corinthian Christians to put their spiritual gifts to use on earth for the life of the neighbor. Jesus put it even more strongly in his parable of the day of judgment. Those who were judged fit for the kingdom sat on his right hand. They had seen Jesus hungry and fed him, thirsty and gave him drink, a stranger and welcomed him and so forth. But these great saints were shocked. "When did we do that for you, Jesus? We don't remember." (Saints are always the last to know their own goodness!) Jesus answered, " . . . as you did it to one of the least of these my brethren, you did it to me" (Matt. 25:40). Catch the full meaning of Jesus' words! When we serve the humblest person on earth, *we serve Jesus*. Humble and ordinary service to God's creation and God's creatures is very spiritual work. Gifts of the Spirit are as broad as God's creation itself.

> 6. *Justification and Sanctification are two ways of picturing a single reality.*
> But you were washed, you were sanctified, you were justified in the name of the Lord Jesus Christ and in the Spirit of our God (1 Cor. 6:11).

Most Christians assume that justification and sanctification refer to two different phases of God's work with his people. Justification is phase one. Condemnation for sin is removed. That is the beginning. The continuation of what has begun, phase two, is sanctification or Christian growth. Sometimes justification is associated with the work of Jesus and sanctification with the work of the Spirit.

This distinction is made in many books of theology and religion. I question, however, if it is a legitimate biblical distinction. What we need to understand is the role in God's one life-giving work which justification and sanctification (and redemption, reconciliation, and adoption!) play. These words are metaphors, each with its own shade of meaning, which point to a single reality. That reality is the reality of the gospel which is simply too great a reality to be contained in a single metaphor. In the passage quoted above, for example, sanctification and justification stand side by side describing the one deed of God.

Justification is a metaphor taken from the forum of the law court. Someone stands guilty before the judge. Unexpectedly someone else appears and makes his case good. He is justified. The condemnation for his sin and guilt is taken away. (See Rom. 8:1). That is one way of picturing the work of God in Christ. He justifies guilty people.

Sanctification is a metaphor taken from the Old Testament world of ritual. The words sanctify, sanctified and sanctification occur three times more often in the Old Testament than in the New. People, altars, fields, tabernacles and priests are unclean (unholy) until God sets them apart for his service. God's *setting-apart* action is called sanctification. When we use the word sanctification to refer to God's action in Christ we are saying that God sets us apart, makes us holy. Those touched by God's work are set apart, clean, holy, saints. That is another picture which tries to capture the meaning of God's saving deed in Christ.

In both of these pictures God is seen as the actor and *people* as the passive receivers of God's action. God acts to justify the guilty. God acts to sanctify the unclean. We are justified and we are sanctified because of what God has done for us in Christ. "He is the source of your life in Christ Jesus, whom God made our wisdom, our righteousness and sanctification and redemption" (1 Cor. 1:30). Note how Paul heaps us his metaphors. The word *righteousness* used in this passage is a term very close to the word *justi-*

*fication* in meaning. The Spirit is the present tense power of justification and sanctification. The Spirit works through Word and sacrament to justify us in the midst of our guilt. The Spirit works through Word and sacrament to sanctify us from all of our impurities and uncleanness.

Justification and sanctification are terms that refer to the Spirit's work within us. Neither term refers to a reality which is our own, which belongs to us. Justification and sanctification are alien and foreign to our being. They are the Spirit's gifts to us. Alien justification—alien sanctification. These are the Spirit's realities in our life even when we do not see clear evidences of their presence. We are justified/sanctified by faith, not by sight.

Once again, the passage which always haunts me in this connection is Matthew 25:31-46. It is the story where the Son of man comes in glory to separate the sheep from the goats. He separates them. Those who are at his right hand marvel at their selection. The Lord said they were there because they saw *him* in the needs of the hungry and thirsty and naked and imprisoned and cared for him. With one voice they replied, "Lord, when did we see thee a stranger and welcome thee?" (See verses 37-38.) They could not believe their own holiness! They could not remember doing these deeds of kindness and love. Their holiness was so alien to their being that they did not even know what they were doing. That's what a New Testament saint looks like. He doesn't know his own saintliness.

Justification and sanctification should not be understood as static realities. The gospel proclaims, "You are justified! You are sanctified!" Justification and sanctification become realities in our life the moment we hear those words and believe them. We *are* justified. We *are* sanctified. We are justified/sanctified because God says so. God then works through our entire life making what he has called reality, an actual reality. We *are* justified/sanctified. But we are also *being* justified/sanctified as an ongoing process of God. God began a good work in us. He promises to complete what he began. "And I am sure that he who began a good work in you will bring it to completion at the day of Jesus Christ" (Phil. 1:6).

There is, therefore, growth into justification and growth into sanctification. We should be aware, however, of the nature of that growth. Christian growth does not refer to the increase in our observable piety and goodness. Never! Christian growth refers to the growth of the Spirit's work in our lives. The Spirit grows and moves forward. We die and move backwards. Christ lives. We die. That's Christian growth. That's justification/sanctification in the process of actualization. We seldom know what Christ is doing in and through us in this actualization process. That's a secret kept from us. But God knows. God knows his saints. God knows what you and I don't know. Our justification/sanctification is alien to us, but not to God.

*Application:* Neo-Pentecostals, following the classic Pentecostal tradition, often understand the gifts of the Spirit as part of the process of sanctification. In this understanding those who possess spiritual gifts may assume that those gifts are steps along the way to a fuller, more mature Christian life. Those who are in sympathy with this position but who seem to possess none of the gifts often take that as a sign that they have not grown and matured in Christ as they ought to have. Some of the signs of sanctification are missing in their life and experience. Many people are very concerned with their own spirituality because of this. "If only I could be baptized in the Spirit, then I would feel like I'm getting off dead center in my Christian life." I've heard that sentiment expressed quite often.

It's extremely logical to believe that lack of spiritual gifts means a lack of Christian growth and sanctification. Logical, but is it correct? I seriously doubt it! Justification and sanctification should not be separated in such a way that gifts of the Spirit are referred to our sanctification. When we separate justification from sanctification in this manner we tend to think of justification as *God's* job and sanctification as *our* job (even though we usually give credit to the Holy Spirit). Sanctification, however, is not our job. It, too, is God's job. It's the Holy Spirit's job. Both justification and sanctification are God's job with us. These words are simply different ways of describing the fact that God seeks to make us his children and rule in our lives.

Sanctification is a word that points to God's growing rule over our lives. With our physical eyes we have a tough time measuring God's growing rule in us. In fact, we can't do it. We can measure our work. That's easy. We can measure how we think our lives ought to look to God. God obviously wants lives that are spiritually gifted! At this point a real temptation sets in. It is the temptation for the gifted ones to claim that the Spirit's gifts are sure signs of their Christian growth and sanctification. Gifts of the Spirit in this interpretation become signs by which we may know, see and measure our spiritual growth.

That's one way of understanding spiritual gifts. It's dangerous, however. Spiritual gifts, in this understanding, become the signs of our saintliness. Our saintliness, however, is not something we know. Our saintliness is alien to

our being. We don't know we are saints. We *believe* that
we are. We believe it often *in spite of,* not because of, the
observable evidence.

"Believed" saintliness is what Luther meant by his para-
doxical statement that a Christian is *simultaneously a saint
and a sinner.* We are not 60 percent saint and 40 percent
sinner or 75 percent saint and 25 percent sinner. Such per-
centing always leaves us with the impression that our per-
centage of sinfulness is something *we* must overcome. There
are no such percentages! It's always 100 percent sinner and
100 percent saint at the same time. In and of ourselves we
are 100 percent sinful. Because of what God has done for us
we are 100 percent saints. Our sinfulness is our own. Our
saintliness is God's gift to us. It is alien to our being. It's
always sinners who are saints. We can't figure that out.
God can. He makes it happen.

With reference to gifts of the Spirit this means it is always *sinners* who possess those gifts. Always sinners! Spiritual gifts are not the natural outgrowth of our sanctification. They are gifts of God which are always alien to our
nature. Spiritual gifts are alien to us. They are not ours.
They don't mark our progress. They are the work of God
in people who never deserve such a work. Spiritual gifts
are alien gifts. Language concerning these gifts should
never, therefore, be language about people and their growth.
It should always be language about God and his unbelievable grace.

7. *The Church is the visible gathering of the invisibly
   pious (sinners).*
   Paul, called by the will of God to be an apostle of
   Christ Jesus . . . to the church of God which is at
   Corinth, to those sanctified in Christ Jesus (1 Cor.
   1:1-2).

There are not many of us, had we known the problems of the church at Corinth, that would have addressed them as the sanctified ones. Paul did. For Paul the visible gathering of God's people were the saints of God. In the third biblical foundation above ("God's Spirit is present in outer, visible signs") I maintained that the presence of God in the midst of his people is a visible presence. A church (in Corinth or Columbus) is God's church because of God's visible presence in Word and sacrament; not because of the visible piety of its members. One of the Lutheran church's doctrinal statements (the Augsburg Confession, Article viii) puts it very simply: "The Church is the communion of saints in which the gospel is rightly preached and the sacraments rightly administered."

We need to take great care, therefore, in what we label as visible and what we label as invisible in the Christian life. The *visible* label goes on the church. The church is the visible place where Christians expect God's Spirit to be at work in the public proclamation of the gospel and the public administration of the sacraments. The church: visible.

The *invisible* label goes on the people and their holiness. The holiness of fellow members of Christ's body often seems to be hidden from our eyes. Were the problematic Christians at Corinth really saints? Are those we gather together with on Sunday morning really God's saints? Sometimes that doesn't seem possible to us. The whole idea is alien to us and to our understanding of holiness and saintliness. Alien sanctification. That's what we have called it.

As we have indicated it is always the saints themselves that are more surprised at God's declaration of their holiness than anyone else. No wonder we are admonished by Jesus not to judge (Matt. 7:1). We cannot judge the holiness of others. All that we can see is their outer works. Salvation, however, is not by works but by grace alone. Only God knows who really trusts him above all things. We see the outer side, the works. He sees the inner side, the heart. The saints: invisible.

Consider the parable Jesus told as reported in Luke 18:9-14. There was a Pharisee. He considered himself to be righteous. He knew his own holiness. So did everyone else. It was obvious. It was visible. Visible piety. The tax collector, on the other hand, only knew his unholiness. Certainly everyone else knew it too. He couldn't even lift up his eyes to God to pray. Meekly he mumbled, "God, be merciful to me a sinner!" (Luke 18:13).

Which one of these men did Jesus bless? It never seems to be the one we think it should be! Concerning the tax collector he said, "I tell you this man went down to his house justified rather than the other; for every one who exalts himself will be humbled, but he who humbles himself will be exalted" (Luke 18:14). Grace alone makes us to be the people of God. The Pharisee saw no need for God's grace. The tax collector did.

*Application:* A Baptist charismatic once addressed a gathering of Lutheran charismatics. He was upset with them and said something like this. "I've talked with many of you the past few days. Usually I've asked you where you go to church. Your answers disturb me. Inevitably you tell me, 'Well, I belong to St. Mark's, or St. Luke's or Resurrection Lutheran but I get my real nourishment from this prayer meeting or that prayer meeting outside of my local congregation.' I want to tell you," he continued, "that you are out of God's order. You belong in your local congregation."

Pastors have told me similar stories. One told of some neo-Pentecostal families in his congregation that found their fellowship outside of the congregation to be the source of strength they needed in order to "put up" with his ministry!

A common cry among some neo-Pentecostals is that their local congregation and pastor are "dead." The pastor doesn't have the Spirit. The people are not "alive." The whole place is a spiritual desert. Where shall they turn? Who will feed them?

What is at issue here is our understanding of the nature of the church. Spiritualists of every age prefer to reverse the labels that I have referred to. The visible church, they say, is filled with hypocrites and sinners. The true church, therefore, is invisible. It consists of those who are visibly pious and holy. So the labels are turned around. The church gets the invisible label. The saints get the visible label. The church is defined as the invisible communion of those whose spirituality and piety is visible for all to see. I have maintained that the opposite position is more closely attuned to the New Testament. The church is the visible gathering of the invisibly pious.

This definition of the church applies also to the matter of spiritual gifts. Spiritual gifts cannot be understood as the visible marks upon those who have been raised above the common lot. Spiritual gifts don't raise us to some special level of spirituality. They are given for the body of Christ: the church. (Remember 1 Cor. 12.) They are for the common good, not the private elevation of a few. Gifts of the

Spirit, therefore, should lead us into the life of the local congregation, not away from it.

The church, the local congregation, the visible assembly of Christians, is always the place where sinners gather. Jesus said "I came not to call the righteous, but sinners" (Mark 2:17). Those who think they are righteous, visibly, often claim to have no need for the visible church. They are probably right. Jesus has no message for them. Jesus' message is one public and visible message for sinners only. "Your sins are forgiven," he says. The public proclamation of that word of good news in Word and sacrament is what makes the church the church.

## Summary

We have tried to set an understanding of spiritual gifts into a broad perspective of biblical foundations. Each of our situations, of course, is different. Each spiritual gift is different. Each of us is different. However, we do need some guidelines for understanding. Let me summarize simply the main points I have made concerning spiritual gifts.

1. Gifts of the Spirit are always gifts in the sense that the gospel is a gift. They are never earned or deserved.

2. Gifts of the Spirit are signs that God is at work in his own way and his own time fashioning us into the likeness of his Son.

3. Gifts of the Spirit come from the Spirit of God who works among us in public signs of Word and Sacrament.

4. Gifts of the Spirit include daily tasks of simple service to our neighbors who share with us the world that God continually creates and redeems.

5. Gifts of the Spirit are alien to our being. They serve to remind us that God's work of justification and sanctification is a work hidden from our eyes.

6. Gifts of the Spirit lead us to service in the life of our local congregation which is our particular link to Christ's body, the church. This corporate or communal aspect of the gifts of the Spirit cannot be overemphasized!

Two other guidelines for understanding the Spirit's gifts will be discussed at the close of Chapter 9, "The Gifts of the Spirit and the Cross of Christ." It may be helpful to include them in this summary list as well:

7. Gifts of the Spirit are given to ʾedify us that we may mutually edify others. Spiritual gifts are given to the community through individuals.

8. Love is the greatest gift of the Spirit.

# 6

# The Kingdom Within

We emerge from the teacher's workshop. I have tried to set forth the biblical foundations for my own understanding of spiritual gifts. My understandings do not necessarily agree with the understandings and interpretations of others who have been involved in the neo-Pentecostal movement. I have many friends, clergy and laity, who have been touched by the neo-Pentecostal phenomena whose interpretation of spiritual experience sometimes differs from mine. One reason for this is that few Protestant churches have offered theological help for interpreting spiritual experience. Lutheran neo-Pentecostals, for example, seldom know how to interpret their experiences in the light of their own tradition. The same is true of other denominations.

In the absence of good interpretative data a phenomenon like speaking in tongues often happens to people in a theological vacuum. They don't know how to interpret that experience. They look for help in the interpretative process. Many books, pamphlets, and tapes are available. What explanatory lens do these materials look through in seeking to understand the meaning of spiritual experience in general and gifts of the spirit in particular? In my opinion two schemes of interpretation dominate the horizon and both of them stand in significant conflict with what I have suggested as biblical foundations.

The first of these interpretive schemes grows naturally out of the change in American culture in the past decade. It seeks to understand the spiritual as the equivalent of our interiority, inwardness, and "within." This chapter will seek to analyze this interpretation.

The second dominant interpretative scheme is the theological interpretation of spiritual experience worked out in the Pentecostal churches. This approach will be analyzed in the next chapter.

## American Cultural Change

American life and culture has been dominated from its birth by the intellectual movement often referred to as the Enlightenment. The Enlightenment is characterized, among other things, by its rational, scientific, and objective approach to truth. Truth is something objective. It is "out there" to be found and tested by all who apply proper scientific methodology.

The intellectual movement that challenges this Enlightenment mentality is called Romanticism. Romanticism is characterized by subjectivity. Truth is not something "out there" to be analyzed, classified and pigeonholed. Truth is something "in here." Truth is "within" me. I am the subject of truth. Truth is not discovered by searching the great world around us for objective answers. Truth is found by searching the great world *within* the self. The answers are subjective. They are my answers.

Romantic themes dominated the youth revolution of the late 1960s and the early 1970s. Popular music was filled with these themes. The shifting mood of students could easily be described as a shift from an Enlightenment to a Romantic perspective. Students who were once "into" social and political issues are now "into" themselves in a variety of ways. The drug culture, the "Jesus Movement," the appeal of Eastern religions, mysticism, and the occult are all signs of a movement *into the self*. Truth is not "out there" in social and political revolution. Truth is "in here," within my own being. A publishing phenomena of the early 1970s was *Jonathan Livingston Seagull*. The dedication of that work reads, "To the Jonathan Livingston Seagull (the bird that overcomes all obstacles) *within* us all" (Italics mine).

This can be illustrated most easily by looking at the task of teaching religion to young people today. In 1965 the student mood was such that a teacher of religion sought to show in a *rational* way that there was something in Christianity one could believe in. At the present time the task with young people is almost the precise opposite. Young people today believe in too much. The teacher's task is to point out the boundaries of what one can rightfully believe within the Christian tradition. If truth is really what people find locked within themselves there are a lot of truths! Each person discovers his own truth. In that kind of situation Pilate's ancient question haunts us, "What is truth?"

The shift of truth's location from "out there" to "in here" has had its effect on Christian theology. Most of the influential books on theology written during the first six decades of the 20th century sought to salvage something believable about Christianity from the attacks of science and the critical historians. Some theologians even acknowledged that "God is dead." The critics had won.

In the early '70s theology has experienced some movement from an emphasis on intellect and will to an emphasis on experience and feeling. Sam Keen and Harvey Cox have written theological treatises seeking to support the thesis that truth lies within man. The text for this new theology seems to be taken from a passage which occurs once in the New Testament: " . . . the kingdom of God is within you" (Luke 17:21).

## Morton Kelsey, Carl Jung and the Kingdom Within

In my mind it is highly problematic for people to seek to understand spiritual experiences, including the experiences associated with neo-Pentecostalism, with reference to human interiority. This kind of interpretation however has been worked out in detail by men like Morton Kelsey and Watchman Nee. These authors have a great deal of influence on people who are associated with the neo-Pentecostal revival. Kelsey's book, *Encounter With God,* for example has been called, " . . . the most thoroughly worked-out and documented theology for the charismatic which has been done anywhere."

With this kind of recommendation it is important for us to inquire into Kelsey's "theology of Christian experience." His understanding of spiritual experience can be understood rather clearly from his *Encounter With God*. His concern is to validate, explain, and interpret Christian experience. Working as a disciple of the great Swiss psychiatrist, Carl

Gustav Jung, he seeks to build a world view that can accommodate spiritual experience. Kelsey believes that the theologies we have worked with since the Reformation (Lutheran theology, Reformed theology and so forth) do not include a place for *direct experience* of God.

How, for example, can we understand speaking in tongues if we don't have a theology and a world view that allows for direct experience with God? We need a better lens through which we might interpret our spiritual experience. Kelsey's sincere attempt is to provide such a lens.

Central to his attempt at providing a justification for direct religious experience is his assertion that there are *two equally real worlds of reality.* One world is the *physical* world, with which we have contact through our senses. That is the "out there" world, the world of consciousness. The other equally real world is the *spiritual* world. It is an invisible world and not available to our senses. It is not conscious. It is the world of the unconscious or subconscious. Kelsey maintains that this world, *the spiritual world, is the source of direct religious experiences.* By religious experiences in this statement Kelsey is referring to such things as dreams, healing, extra-sensory perception (ESP), speaking in tongues, prophecy, and clairvoyance.

For Kelsey there are two worlds: physical and spiritual. Conscious and subconscious. One world is available to our body and our senses. Another world is available to our soul and spiritual experience. Though God may confront us through both worlds, *direct* religious experience comes through the spiritual world. God is, so to speak, at the base or foundation of the spiritual world. God is the name we give to the objective center of meaning which lies at the depth of our being, the depth of the universe. It is in the

depth of our being that the worlds of God and man inter-
sect. The depth of our being is the place where we experience and encounter God directly. God is always seeking to
push up through that world and communicate with us.
God pursues us through the spiritual realm. We do not
have to actively seek or pursue him. He is *within* us! All
we need to do is to be open to his presence and allow our
experience with him to happen, says Kelsey.

Direct experience of God is possible for every person.
But such direct experiences of the spiritual world do not
just happen. We must be open to them. Openness means
that our total psyches must go into training. To encounter
the spiritual, we must give ourselves totally to the task.
Kelsey provides *twelve rules* to follow if we wish to participate in direct spiritual experiences.

Rule 1.   Act as though you believe in the spiritual
realm.

Rule 2.   Undertake the quest with serious purpose.

Rule 3.   Seek companionship and spiritual direction
for the spiritual journey.

Rule 4.   Turn away from the busy-ness of the outer
world in silence and introversion.

Rule 5.   Learn the value of genuine fasting.

Rule 6.   Learn to use the forgotten faculty of the
imagination.

Rule 7.   Keep a journal. (This should be done so
you can see the effects of what is happening to you.)

Rule 8.   Record your dreams.

Rule 9.   Be as honest with yourself as you can and
get someone else to help you be honest.

Rule 10.   Let your life manifest real love.

Rule 11.   Gird yourself with persistence and courage.

Rule 12.   Give generously of your material goods.

What would this system mean for the interpretation of spiritual experience? Kelsey has clearly seen a problem in modern theology. The world of spirit and spiritual have often times been sadly neglected. He has sought to correct this imbalance. Has he succeeded? Before I attempt to speak to that question and evaluate Kelsey in the light of my own biblical foundations I would like to sketch just a few of the conclusions that a neo-Pentecostal might reach if he used this system as the interpretative key for his own spiritual experiences.

The basic thrust of Kelsey's approach is that man gets "into" God when he gets "into" himself. Though Kelsey would certainly allow God to be at work in the outer and physical world his strong tendency is to identify God's real presence with the spiritual world and our "within." When we get into ourselves, into the depths of our being, we have experiences of infinite spiritual dimensions. We cross paths with God. We encounter him. Dreams, ESP, and speaking in tongues become signs of that encounter. Such an interpretation means that speaking in tongues bursts forth from the depths of our being; it is our vocalization of the "collective unconscious." If we can tap those depths, the core of self, we can speak in tongues. When we speak in tongues (other phenomenon could be listed as well) we have a sign that we have tapped the core, the depths of self, the experiential intersection with God. Tongues is a sign, therefore, that we have moved experientially closer to God.

Limiting ourselves to the phenomenon of tongues Kelsey provides us with a map to the experience and an interpretation of the experience. Can everyone speak in tongues? Yes, would be his answer. That ability is locked away in the unconscious world within each of us. How do we unlock that "gift?" Adherence to the twelve rules is the best path to follow. If we follow the rules of spiritual training a host of spiritual experiences await us. God lies at the depth of our existence waiting to push through into our consciousness. The spiritual man can be identified as the one who has opened his life to *the kingdom within.*

Tongues is a sign of the outbreaking of that kingdom. Speaking in tongues is a sign that the spiritual world within us has burst into consciousness. The one who speaks in tongues is a person in tune with the spiritual. He has encountered God directly. His tongue is the visible evidence for all to see that spiritual reality is beginning to break through and pervade his being. He who speaks in tongues is clearly close to God. Those who do not evidence this or another sign of their spiritual encounters are not as deeply in tune with *the kingdom within.* Their spiritual journey has not taken them as deeply into the hidden realm. In this system, spiritual experiences can easily be interpreted as *qualitative* signs of a deeper walk with God.

## A Voice from China: Watchman Nee

Another author, widely read in neo-Pentecostal and Pentecostal circles, who has a tendency to understand the human "within" as the contact point for the work of the Spirit of God is the Chinese theologian Watchman Nee. Nee bases his understanding of man on his reading of the Bible. He is particularly impressed with the implications of what it means to be a human person in a passage like 1 Thessalonians 5:23. "May the God of peace himself sanctify you wholly; and may your spirit and soul and body be kept sound and blameless at the coming of our Lord

Jesus Christ." For Nee the implications of such a passage are clear. Man is a three-fold being. He has a spirit and a soul and a body.

The body, in his analysis, is the outer part of man. It is the lowest of the three aspects of humanity for it makes contact with the material world of the senses. Through the body we are conscious of the world around us.

Our soul and spirit dwell within our bodies. The spirit is our innermost part. It is to our bodies what the holy of holies was to the temple in the Old Testament. It is our noblest part for it joins us with God. Our spirit gives us a consciousness of God just as our bodies give us a consciousness of the world. The similarities between this and Kelsey's two equally real worlds, physical and spiritual, are striking.

We are citizens, therefore, of two worlds. We belong to the physical world. Our bodies give us a sense of contact with that world. We also belong to God and the spiritual world. Our spirits give us that consciousness. That which joins our body and our spirit together is the soul. Soul binds body and spirit together. Our soul, according to Nee, is ourself. It is the seat of self-consciousness. It is the "real I". The soul life is the life we inherit at birth.

What is man? He is body, soul, and spirit. The most important of these three parts is the spirit. Nee is concerned above all else that we understand the essence and importance of our spirit. It is our most important part because every communication we have with God occurs there! When we talk about man as a fallen creature, says Nee, we are talking primarily about the fall of the spirit. After the fall, the spirit of Adam died. That means that our spirits are also dead. Apart from the saving work of Christ we are not body, soul and spirit. Apart from that work we are only body and soul. It is only as the first fruit of the resurrection that God gives new birth to our deadened spirits The work of Christ's salvation, therefore, is a work "within" us. Our "within," our spirit, is brought back to life.

The work of the Holy Spirit is also understood as a work within. Christ gives new birth to our within, to our spirit, and the Holy Spirit seeks to gain control over that spirit. The Holy Spirit, in other words, works his work upon us from the *inside out*. Once he has control over our inside, our spirit, he can move out to control our soul and our body as well. All satanic works are performed from the outside inward; all divine works, from the inside outward.

The "inside out" work of the Spirit differs from one Christian to another. Once the Spirit enlivens our spirit and gains control over it he is to work from that within (our inside) in order to give life to soul and body as well. Nee observes that the Spirit does not get that job done equally well for all Christians. Christians, therefore, fall into two classifications. There are spiritual Christians and there are carnal Christians. He bases this distinction on 1 Corinthians 3:1: "But I, brethren, could not address you as spiritual men, but as men of the flesh, as babes in Christ." "Spiritual men" here refers to spiritual Christians. "Men of the flesh" refers to fleshly or carnal Christians. A Spiritual Man (the title of Nee's book) or a spiritual Christian is one whose soul and body are controlled by the working of the Holy Spirit within the human spirit. A carnal Christian is one whose spirit has been brought to life but who still follows his soul and body into sin. Carnal Christians have reborn spirits, they have been forgiven of their sins, but they have not as yet ceased from sin. They, therefore, possess only *half* of God's salvation.

Spiritual Christians, on the other hand, possess *all* of their salvation. They are forgiven and they have overcome sin by the full indwelling of the Spirit of God in their spirit. This full salvation, this total indwelling of the Holy Spirit in the human spirit, does not come naturally or easily. *It requires our cooperation* with the Spirit of God. Jesus is the model of how this cooperation is to be effected. As he was dying, Jesus poured out his soul to death, but committed his spirit to God (Luke 23:46). We must do now what he did before. If we truly pour out the soul life and commit our spirit to God we too shall know the power of resurrection and shall enjoy a perfect spiritual way in the glory of the resurrection.

We must do now what he did before. Jesus is our model and example. Nee, therefore, lists *seven steps* whereby we may arrive at the experience of having Jesus divide our soul from our spirit thus making us spiritual Christians. Briefly these steps are:

1. Know the necessity of having spirit and soul divided

2. Ask for the separation of soul and spirit

3. Yield specifically

4. Stand on Romans 6:11 (and 6:12)

5. Pray and study the Bible

6. Daily bear the cross

7. Live according to the spirit.

These are the conditions which we must fulfill. The Holy Spirit requires this cooperation from us. The Lord will not be able to do his part if we fail to do our part. This particular kind of obedience will lead to our becoming a "spiritual man." Becoming spiritual requires such obedience. Faith is not enough. Faith is the first step. It brings regeneration and forgiveness to our spirit. Regeneration and forgiveness, however, are insufficient. They are the marks of the carnal Christian. Only true obedience which follows faith can bring us to the point of becoming spiritual Christians.

Watchman Nee's "spiritual man" is a man whose body and soul are totally controlled by the Holy Spirit through the new-born human spirit. True spirituality flows from the inside out. I am not interested in presenting the entire theological system of Watchman Nee. I am interested, however, in his tendency, like that of Morton Kelsey, to identify man's deepest interiority (spirit) as the location of the communication that God has with us. The Holy Spirit speaks to and through our innermost spirit. God makes contact with us in the innermost depths of our being. The kingdom of God touches us "within."

## Critical Analysis

It is my contention that the tendency to equate human inwardness with the Christian understanding of the "spiritual" as it is done by Morton Kelsey and Watchman Nee is unbiblical and that it provides a dangerous groundwork for the understanding and interpretation of the work of the Spirit and spiritual gifts. Such an interpretation runs counter to at least four biblical foundations.

1. *Salvation is by grace alone.* It seems clear to me that when we identify the presence of God with our "within" or relate it significantly to our "within" that grace is not alone. The fullness of God's grace then only becomes available to those who go into spiritual training and keep the

*twelve rules* or to those who are obedient to the *seven steps* that Jesus modeled for us. But as soon as one adds twelve rules or seven steps to our relationship with God and his Spirit it becomes quite clear that grace is not *alone*. Both Kelsey and Nee are really talking about grace *plus*. It is grace *plus* human openness. It is grace *plus* obedience to the rules and the steps. It is grace *plus* man's plunge within and into himself.

As soon as grace takes on any *plus* it becomes an endless spiral of more and more human endeavor. If spiritual experiences come as a direct result of keeping the twelve rules and being a spiritual man is dependent on our cooperative keeping of the seven steps then the more we keep the rules (and the more rules we keep!) the more spiritual experiences we will have. If spiritual experiences cease it is a sign that we have lapsed in our efforts. We should have been more serious about the quest. We should try more silence, more introversion, more discipline in separating spirit from soul, more energy towards becoming spiritual, more honesty, more love, more giving, and so on and on and on. More! That's Satan's favorite word. Only grace *alone* rescues us from the endless clutches of that tempting *more*. Only grace alone calms our troubled and guilty conscience as we read men like Kelsey and Nee and their programs for spiritual improvement.

This "more" thinking also creates difficulty for our understanding of spiritual gifts. The New Testament talks of speaking in tongues and other spiritual experiences as *gifts* of the Spirit. The temptation in interpretations like that of Kelsey and Nee is to understand spiritual experiences as a *reward* for spiritual openness and obedience. Spiritual experiences are the reward for human openness to the kingdom within. Becoming a "spiritual man" is the reward of our obedience in following Jesus' example and model. We must be clear on this point. Whatever happens to us in the realm of spiritual experience, the gifts of the spirit for example, is *either* a gift freely given *or* a reward for our openness and obedience. Either/or. It cannot be both.

2. *God's Spirit is present to man in outer, visible signs.* God comes to our inner self, our "within," from his "without." The entire witness of biblical history is that God intervenes in the outward course of human events. See for example Hebrews 1:1-4. God assaults and invades our "within" as he moves into our lives from his own realm. This movement is not invisible but visible. The visible and public climax of God's movement toward us was the incarnation. The visible and public extensions of the incarnation in our midst today are the Word and the sacraments (words, water, bread, and wine).

God moves to our "within" from his "without." The tendency in the understanding of God and Spirit in both Kelsey and Nee is to identify the presence of God with our "within" and to minimize the importance and impact of God's "withoutness." Luther sometimes liked to refer to God's presence as that of "outer outerness." The God revealed in the Bible is a God of "outer outerness." He comes from his world outside of our existence and transforms the entire realm of our existence. He transforms us, body and soul.

We do not, therefore, discover or find God at the depths of of our being, in our own interiority, within ourselves. We do not find God "in here," so to speak. We find and discover God "out there." He comes to us in the visible and public stuff of Word and sacrament. That is where we encounter God's Spirit. The promise of God's presence is attached to visible signs in our midst. He gracefully and freely gives himself and his gifts in and through these outer, visible signs. We don't become spiritual people by entering into the depths of our own invisible being. We become spiritual people by being encountered by God and his Spirit as he encounters us again and again through the outer outerness of words and bread and wine and people.

3. *Spirit versus flesh refers to the struggle between God and man.* Spirit refers to God as he opposes our human rebelliousness. Rebelliousness is of the flesh. It is precisely man's *innermost within* that rebels against God! To live according to the flesh is to live for self and away from God. To live according to the Spirit is to accept life as God's gift.

Kelsey and Nee tend to understand the battle between Spirit and flesh (body/physical/matter) to be a struggle between man's interior spiritual self and his exterior physical self. The inner self is in direct communication with God and seeks to bring the outer self (soul and body in Nee) under control. Sin is not understood as that which effects our whole being. Sin effects only the bodily/physical part of man. By tuning in to the interior reality of our lives we can bring the exterior reality of life under control as well. We shall no longer be carnal, fleshly Christians but spiritual Christians.

How we would like to believe that! We would no longer need to confess that we are "by nature sinful and unclean." We would reach into our great within, keep the twelve rules, follow the seven steps, cooperate with the Holy Spirit, have direct spiritual experiences and grow daily in Christian maturity. Our egos really get excited about that

kind of message. Our spirits will conquer our flesh. Our
within will conquer our without. That message is much
more to the liking of our ego (our within) than the message that God's Spirit must crush our whole being in order
to raise up new life within.

It's more to our liking, but it does not have much to do
with the New Testament. There we read that salvation is
a process through which God puts to death our body *and*
soul, our without *and* within, our "out there" *and* our "in
here" and conforms us to the likeness of the new man,
Jesus Christ. We must die. Every part of our being must
die. He must live. The Spirit of God struggles daily with
us to put us to death. It is a tough struggle. We don't want
to die. We want to live. We want to live through the law.
We want to keep the rules and the commandments and
the steps and proclaim our spiritual growth factors for the
whole world to hear. That's what we want. But that's not
the way it is. "For I through the law died to the law, that
I might live to God. I have been crucified with Christ; it
is no longer I who live, but Christ who lives in me; and
the life I now live in the flesh I live by faith in the Son
of God, who loved me and gave himself for me" (Gal.
2:19-20).

4. *Justification and sanctification are two ways of picturing a single reality.* God's work with us, whether it is described as justification or as sanctification, points to his
*single* work of putting our self to death and bringing us
out of death to new life in Christ. Kelsey and Nee clearly
present for us what can happen when justification and
sanctification are understood as different realities. Kelsey,
for example, could easily define sanctification in terms of
advanced spiritual experience. As we follow the rules and

get in touch with our spiritual "within," spiritual experiences result. Such experiences, speaking in tongues for example, are then interpreted as qualitative signs of a deep walk with the inner spirit. Spiritual experiences are easily identified as the signs of *our* (note the "our") sanctification, growth, and maturity.

Nee plainly sets forth a doctrine of a double standard among Christians. There are carnal Christians and there are spiritual Christians. Carnal Christians may be justified, their sins are forgiven, but they are not sanctified. Spiritual Christians, on the other hand, possess *both* justification and sanctification. The sign of their sanctification is the conquest of sin in their lives.

When sanctification is understood as an advanced stage of Christian maturity, when sanctification is understood as something different from justification, several problems arise. People begin to be proud of their advanced spirituality. Some Christians look down on other Christians. All of us feel deep guilt pangs over the low estate of our own sanctification. In the judgment that goes on between Christians over who is and who is not truly sanctified the nerve center of Christian community is shattered. It is a tragedy when the good news that God loves sinners is hidden behind human attempts to improve on what God has begun and continues in our lives. God's first word to us is that he loves us in spite of ourselves. God's last word to us is that he loves us in spite of ourselves. Any understanding of spirituality (sanctification) which moves us from total dependence on God's gracious good news is a misunderstanding of the meaning of spirituality.

I have tried to show the dangers of interpreting spiritual experiences in relation to the kingdom within us. The interpretations of spiritual experience given by Morton Kelsey and Watchman Nee are well known to many Pentecostals and neo-Pentecostals. I believe that they are problematic interpretations of the meaning of Christian experience.

Another framework for interpreting Christian experiences, like speaking in tongues, is that framework proposed by classic Pentecostalism. Many neo-Pentecostals are unconsciously influenced by this framework. In the next chapter we shall try to clarify and analyze Pentecostal theology.

# 7

# Pentecostal Theology:
# Evidence of the Spirit

*And the believers from among the circumcised who
came with Peter were amazed, because the gift of the
Holy Spirit had been poured out even on the Gentiles. For they heard them speaking in tongues (Acts
10:45-46).*

Experience is a valid fact of life for Christians. Conversion, prayer, worship, and tongues are genuine forms of
Christian experience. When experience is interpreted, however, we move from experience to theology. I have offered
a series of biblical foundations as a way of understanding
spiritual experience. Morton Kelsey and Watchman Nee
offer an alternative interpretive framework. Classic Pentecostal theology offers still another method for interpreting
spiritual experience.

Consciously or unconsciously, themes from the Pentecostal interpretative method have pervaded the neo-Pentecostal movement. Neo-Pentecostals do not have a ready-
made framework for understanding the phenomenon of
glossolalia. Pentecostalism does. Christians new to this

experience often lean heavily on this existent interpretive framework to understand their own experience. The majority of questions people ask me concerning neo-Pentecostalism have been influenced by Pentecostal ideas. Usually those who ask these questions are not aware of this influence. Neo-Pentecostals, in general, are not knowledgeable of Pentecostal theology or of its pervasive influence on their own thinking. It is important, therefore, to understand classic Pentecostalism. What is presented here, obviously is only a skeletal outline of that thought. For a detailed presentation and critique of Pentecostal theology by a renowned Pentecostal theologian, see Walter J. Hollenweger's *The Pentecostals,* published by Augsburg Publishing House.

## The Acts of the Apostles as the Heart of the New Testament

Pentecostalism was born in America at the outset of the 20th century. Landmarks of its origin are the Topeka Revival around 1901 and the Los Angeles Revival in 1906. The Los Angeles revival was headed by W. J. Seymour who proclaimed that speaking in tongues was the sign of a Spirit-filled Christian. As his work grew and people began to manifest the spiritual evidence of tongues he located his operation in an old Methodist Church on Azusa Street in Los Angeles. The present worldwide movement of Pentecostalism regards this Azusa Street Mission as its origin.

Pentecostalism arose around an experience: speaking in tongues. Pentecostal theology has been a theology in search of an explanation and interpretation of that experience. The search ended with the re-discovery of the book of Acts. Pentecostal theology is basically an interpretation of that single book of the New Testament. We began this chapter with a quotation from Acts. It is a passage which seems to imply that speaking in tongues is a sign or evidence of the presence of the Holy Spirit. That is the basic declaration of Pentecostal theology. Speaking in tongues is understood to be the *initial evidence* of the baptism in the Spirit.

Pentecostal theology tends to read the New Testament evidence in the light of the book of Acts. It is the heart of the New Testament in their understanding. It is the pivotal center of the whole. The Gospels serve as an introduction to Acts. They prophesy that the Spirit will be poured out. The Epistles reflect the fall-out of the experience of the day of Pentecost. They are a postscript to Acts. The Gospels are introduction, the Epistles a postscript. The book of Acts is the center. That's the Pentecostal method of interpreting the New Testament.

This means that Acts presents us with the actual record of how life was lived in the early church. For the Pentecostal, it is the obligatory model for all subsequent generations. Life and experience in the church today ought to be a copy of the life and experiences of the first Christians. The inauguration of that life was the event of the day of Pentecost when the disciples were filled with the Holy Spirit and began to speak in other tongues (Acts 2:1-11). Other passages in Acts that mention speaking in tongues are used to support this point for them. What was true for the first disciples must be true for us. We, too, should be filled with the Holy Spirit. The sign, proof or evidence of that infilling is glossolalia. According to the central book of the New Testament the full Christian life is marked by an initial sign: speaking in tongues. The Pentecostal implication of this for 20th Century Christians is clear!

## Salvation in Two Stages

The theological implications of Acts are not agreed upon by all Pentecostals. Pentecostal sects differ from each other. At the heart of all their interpretations, however, is the division of God's work of salvation with the believer into stages. Some divide that work into two stages: justification and sanctification. There are ordinary Christians (justification) and Spirit-filled Christians who evidence their sanctification through the sign of tongues. Other Pentecostals speak of three stages. First, we are converted. Secondly, we are sanctified. Thirdly, we receive the baptism in the Spirit with the initial evidence of tongues. Resolution of this different placement of tongues (is it the second or third stage in the believer's growth?) is the most serious internal theological problem facing Pentecostal theology today.

We can attempt to explain the primary motifs of the two-stage theory with the help of the following diagram:

| *Stage One* | | *Stage Two* |
|---|---|---|
| 1. Christ | → | 1. Holy Spirit |
| 2. Sinners | → | 2. Saints |
| 3. Justification | → | 3. Sanctification |
| 4. First Faith | → | 4. Second (Total) Faith |
| 5. Water Baptism | → | 5. Spirit Baptism |
| RESULT: An urge for *more*. Doctrine of Conditions. | | RESULT: *Tongues* as the initial evidence. |

This diagram represents two different phases or stages in the life of the believer before God. In the first stage,

according to Pentecostal thinking, we make contact with
1. *Christ*. Christ died for 2. *sinners*. Christ's death for sinners is known as 3. *justification*. Such is the work of Christ.
He died that sinners might no longer be condemned under
God's law but that they might be justified before God by
the blood of Christ.

Justification, therefore, is a reality for all who have
4. *faith* ("first faith") in the justifying work of Christ's
blood shed for their sins. As a testimony to God and the
community that we have believed we receive 5. *water baptism*. This water baptism corresponds to John the Baptist's
baptism of repentance. Water baptism is the believer's initial (first faith) witness to the fact that he believes in the
justifying work of the blood of Christ.

The result of these five-steps in stage one is an intense
desire on the part of the believer for *more*. (There's that
word again.) Justified sinners, after all, are still sinners! No
"true" Christian will be satisfied with that fact. A Christian
cannot be satisfied with being a sinner, with first faith,
with water baptism. There is *more*. Every "true" Christian
knows that and yearns for that *more*. He yearns to be a
stage two, not just a stage one, Christian!

But how does that happen? How do we get from stage
one to stage two? Pentecostal theories vary. Most set
forth some kinds of conditions for the believers to meet
in order that they might move onward and upward in
their Christian life and existence. A universal condition is
that the Christian must put away all *known* sin. Many
other conditions may be listed. Though Pentecostal works
of theology vary at this point it is apparent that in the final
analysis *man is the prime active agent* in the move from

stage one to stage two. If man meets the conditions, if he has total faith, if he is totally yielded and open to God, he can become a stage two Christian.

Stage two, you will notice begins with the work of the 1. *Holy Spirit*. Pentecostal theology, therefore, separates the work of Christ from the work of the Spirit. Christ and the Spirit are two separate persons of the Trinity with two separate works to do. Christ works to justify sinners. The Spirit works to sanctify 2. *saints*. Cause and effect are sometimes difficult to determine at this point in Pentecostal theology. Does the Spirit cause us to become saints? Or, do we become saints ourselves by meeting the conditions, thereby qualifying for the Spirit's work and gifts? The latter seems to be the case. Becoming saints, becoming 3. *sanctified* is our task. That this is the case is clear from the often-stated Pentecostal position that the Spirit cannot dwell in the same heart where sin dwells. Christ can be with us while we are yet sinners. The Spirit, however, can only come to live with us fully when we have removed all known sin from our lives.

There are two kinds of Christians. There are stage one Christians and stage two Christians. The difference is up to us. We can transfer ourselves from the realm of Christ to the realm of Spirit. We can overcome sin and become saints. We can move from justification to sanctification. We can exercise a second and totally complete faith. First faith is insufficient. It is insufficiently directed and insufficiently total. That is because it is not directed towards the full appropriation of the Spirit. This misdirection can be remedied. We can achieve a total faith and a total obedience. Then we will arrive!

The sign that we have arrived at stage two is 5. *Spirit Baptism*. Spirit baptism, which *results* in speaking in tongues as an initial proof or evidence, is the Holy Spirit's way of letting us and the whole community know that we are stage two Christians. Through this Spirit baptism (note there are two baptisms) the Holy Spirit dwells in the believer personally and fully. Spirit baptism with the initial evidence of speaking in tongues is the heart of the Pentecostal experience. It is fitting, therefore, that it be the climactic fact of their theology.

We have now seen the interpretative framework, the theological lens, through which the experience of tongues is understood and interpreted in Pentecostal theology. Speaking in tongues is the initial evidence that a Christian has been baptized for the second time. He has been baptized in the Spirit. Spirit baptism is a sign that he has moved from Christ's primary work of conversion to the Spirit's secondary work of sanctification. It is a sign that he has driven sin out of his life. It is a sign that his faith is total. It is a sign that the Spirit of God now lives personally and fully within him. Speaking in tongues is the Spirit's confirmation of his growth and maturation in the Christian life. It is merit-badge proof that he has arrived at a deeper walk with God.

The scriptural evidence for this interpretation comes, as indicated, from the book of Acts along with other selected passages. One important passage is Hebrews 13:8: "Jesus Christ is the same yesterday and today and forever." Pentecostals interpret this to mean that what happened yesterday (the day of Pentecost with the manifestation of tongues) should happen today.

## Walter Hollenweger's The Pentecostals
## An Internal Criticism

Before examining the Pentecostal framework for interpreting spiritual experience in the light of my biblical foundations, let us list a few of the criticisms leveled at traditional Pentecostal theology by the internationally respected scholar, Walter Hollenweger. Hollenweger has only recently severed his formal ties with the Pentecostal church. His criticisms are basically those of an insider. A few of his criticisms will be given briefly and not necessarily in the order of their importance.

First, Hollenweger is critical of the interpretation and importance assigned to the book of Acts by Pentecostals. He calls such biblical interpretation outdated and obsolete. Acts cannot be understood to be the heart of the New Testament.

Secondly, he points out that any doctrine of stages (two or three) takes away from man any *certainty* of salvation. *More* is always asked of the Christian. If he reaches the second stage he is called to a third stage. If he reaches the third stage someone is there to call him to a higher stage. There is always *more*. Hollenweger states that those outside of the Pentecostal movement cannot begin to comprehend the anguish and guilt caused in Pentecostal Christians through this constant call to the next stage. The solution he proposes is that Pentecostals must learn what it means to live by *grace alone!*

Thirdly, he is critical of the Pentecostal concentration on speaking in tongues. We need to look beyond the traditional gifts of the Spirit to modern gifts of the Spirit such as gifts of service to society and science.

Fourthly, he warns that speaking in tongues cannot be regarded as a self-validating gift. Speaking in tongues, in and of itself, is not necessarily a sign of the work and presence of the Holy Spirit. In some cases non-Christians have spoken in tongues. Hollenweger, therefore, proposes that tongues be validated through their *function*. If they function in people and in the church in such a way that human life becomes the kind of life God intended for us in creation, they are valid. If they create spiritual disease in people they are invalid. Salvation means health. Speaking in tongues should contribute to the task of bringing health to humanity.

Hollenweger indicates that Christians should probably not look to Pentecostalism for a system of *answers*. The importance of Pentecostalism, says Hollenweger, lies in the *questions* it raises, not in the answers it offers. The biggest question raised by Pentecostalism is the question of the *role of the Holy Spirit* in Christian life and faith. Not many Christians have a clear understanding of the work of the Holy Spirit. There is an almost embarrassing lack of clarity and precision in most discussions of the Holy Spirit. Pentecostalism forces us to come to terms with this embarrassment.

Pentecostalism also raises the question of *the place of experience* in Christian life. Pentecostalism is an experience. Its theology can be criticized fairly easily. But what about its experience? What is the role of Christian experience? How do we integrate experience into our theology?

Pentecostal experience is a question to all of us. What they claim as a result of that experience raises more questions. They speak of a power in witness, preaching and mission. Pentecostalism has had considerable missionary success. They speak of a real freedom and spontaneity in worship. Many Christians see Pentecostal worship as full of life when compared to traditional Christian worship.

The list could continue. The point is that many Pentecostal men and women have had experiences in the Christian faith which raise genuine questions for all of us. The mention of women should perhaps be underscored. Women have played an important role in Pentecostalism. Throughout the church's history, Spirit movements have tended to expand the role of women in the church. It is interesting, therefore, to note that in some quarters of the present spiritual awakening women are intentionally excluded from all positions of leadership and authority. In an era of Women's Liberation this is a strange reversal of the role of women in spiritual awakening! My point, however, was about the question raised for us by the experiences of Pentecostal Christians. Pentecostals may need the help of other traditions in theologizing and interpreting those experiences. We, on the other hand, need the help of the Pentecostal Christian in seeking to grasp and glimpse the shape of experience in Christian life.

## Pentecostalism: A Critical Analysis

An analysis of Pentecostal theology in the light of the biblical foundations which I have proposed shows that Pentecostalism stands in opposition to at least four of those foundations.

1. As in the systems proposed by Morton Kelsey and Watchman Nee, Pentecostalism collides with the foundational statement that *salvation is by grace alone*. Each of these interpretative frameworks, in its own way, distorts the meaning of grace alone. We are not debating, there-

fore, on some fringe issues concerning the Christian faith. The heart of the matter is at stake. If we lose the reality of God's gospel of grace alone we don't just lose a particular theological point: we lose everything!

I have mentioned several times that Satan's favorite temptation is the notion that there is *more* to life before God than we (or Adam and Eve) had believed. As far as I can understand it, *more* is a central doctrine in Pentecostal theology. This is not intended to imply that Pentecostal theology is of the devil. However, the meaning of the gospel of grace becomes dangerously obscured.

The doctrine of conditions and the urge for *more* form the bridge in the Pentecostal framework that allows one to cross from the first stage to the second stage of salvation. By meeting the conditions, by doing the *more* that is required, we can move from the realm of Christ to the realm of the Spirit. We can move from sin to holiness. We can move from justification to sanctification, from first faith to total faith, from water baptism to Spirit baptism. One is not called to live by grace alone but is called specifically to live *beyond* the need for grace alone. We are called on to live out of our own strength rather than out of the strength of God's gospel. Speaking in tongues in this system almost becomes a sign that we have moved beyond Christ and his grace for sinners to a higher and more advanced state.

Not all Pentecostals would put the matter that boldly. Most would argue that they believe that a person is saved by grace, but the message that comes through their theology is that there is *more* than grace alone. To live as a sinner saved by grace is not sufficient. There is *more* to Christianity than that. We should not be tempted to follow this path. We live by God's *grace* not man's *more*.

2. Pentecostal theology also runs counter to the foundational statement that *the work of the Holy Spirit is to make the grace of Christ happen in our lives today*. In the New Testament the work of the Holy Spirit is understood as the ongoing presence and activity of Christ's work. The Spirit is the Lord Christ's today-power.

Pentecostal theology also understands the work of the Spirit as today-power. The difference lies in the understanding of the relationship between what happens to us today and what happened in Christ yesterday (when he was alive on earth). Pentecostal theology understands the today-work of the Spirit to be a *different work* from the work of Christ. Christ and the Spirit are different members of the Trinity with different works to do. I am convinced that the New Testament emphasis is that what happens today for us through the power and presence of the Spirit is the *same work* that Christ worked in the past. The Spirit makes Christ's graceful work of love and forgiveness a present reality.

3. Two other biblical foundations that deal with the relation of Christ's work and the Spirit's work, challenge a major thrust of Pentecostal thinking. Those foundational statements were: *The work of the Triune God is one life-giving work;* and *Justification and sanctification are two ways of picturing a single reality*. The cumulative effect of these biblically founded statements is that there is *one* God who has *one* work to do for humanity. These interrelated presuppositions stand in direct opposition to the Pentecostal understanding of *stages*. Their understanding of the stages of salvation, whether two or three, is based on the idea that

each person of the Trinity is distinct and has his own separate work to do. One who claims that God has *one* work with his people is bound to reach some vastly different conclusions about the meaning of Christian life than one who claims that God has *three* works.

God has *one* life-giving work. God the Father created life through his Word (Son) and his breath (Spirit). Man sinned and lost that breath. God loved his creatures and offered to give them life again. God therefore, incarnated life for men in Jesus Christ. "I came that they may have life, and have it abundantly" (John 10:10). The offer of that life is an ongoing offer to us through God's Spirit, the Lord and giver of life. God created life. He incarnated that life in his Son. He recreates that life in us through the present power and work of the Spirit.

The presence of the Spirit among us means that God is a God who continually creates life for us out of the nothingness of our sin and death. In Genesis 1 we read that God created the world out of nothing. That is always how God creates. He continually creates life out of our nothingness. Baptism, in fact, is a sign that God must thrust us into nothingness, into the abyss, into death, to create new life within us.

This stands in marked contrast to a theology that separates the work of Father, Son, and Spirit. In Pentecostal theology justification is regarded as the work of Christ while sanctification is regarded as the work of the Spirit. The major problem with this separation is that it tends to remove us from the all-embracing canopy of God's work for us. This can be seen in the Pentecostal emphasis on holiness (santification). In the final analysis Pentecostalism tends to regard holiness as a human achievement. The

Spirit seals that achievement by baptizing us in the Spirit enabling us to speak in tongues. Tongues is the proof that we have indeed cleansed our hearts from sin, come to a total faith in God, become totally obedient and completely yielded to God.

This is also in contrast to the way holiness is understood when sanctification is thought of as one picture of God's way of working with us. God's works with us are many, yet *one*. He created us. He recreates us. He justifies us. He sanctifies us. Sanctification, holiness, is the result of God's work within us. With respect to holiness each Christian must make a basic decision. Holiness is either God's work in us or our work for God. It is one or the other.

If holiness (sanctification) is our work for God then we are caught up in the endless cycle of *more*. To become holy always requires more of us: more faith, more good works, more obedience, more everything. Until we receive the initial evidence of our holiness, speaking in tongues, we must live under a cloud of guilt over our lack of spiritual achievement. When we do receive the evidence of our holiness we are tempted to be proud of our achievement. Guilt and pride engulf us when holiness is seen as our work for God.

If holiness (sanctification) is God's work in us a completely different response is called for. We are not called on to rise up and live for God. We are called to give up. We are called to turn our feeble efforts over to him. We are called to die to self. We are called to live, trusting simply that God's grace has the transforming power to make us what we can never be out of our own strength—holy. To live trusting our lives entirely into God's hand is to turn our guilt over to God. To acknowledge that God makes us holy in the midst of our unholiness (simultaneously saint and sinner) makes pride over our own spiritual achievements impossible.

The gospel, grace alone, leaves no room for human pride. Grace alone does not call on us to pull ourselves together and become holy. Grace alone calls us to die to ourselves, to our own efforts and our flesh. The gospel calls us to turn from flesh (self) to Spirit. It calls us to live a life of trust in the one work of the Triune God within us.

## Postscript: The Holy Spirit in the Book of Acts

The theology of the Pentecostal churches builds an interpretative framework for understanding spiritual experiences (particularly speaking in tongues) almost entirely on the evidence of the book of Acts. It is important, therefore, to conclude our discussion of Pentecostalism with an examination of the way in which Acts testifies to the work of the Spirit.

The first thing we notice when we read Acts is that the book is about the *continuation of the earthly ministry of Jesus*. Acts 1:1 reads: "In the first book, O Theophilus, I have dealt with all that Jesus *began* to do and teach." The first book referred to is Luke's gospel. Luke's gospel was about the beginnings of Jesus' ministry. Luke's narrative of the life of the early church (Acts) will *continue* that story. Luke proceeds to quote Jesus as telling his disciples to wait for the promise of the Father. Then they shall be "baptized with the Holy Spirit." Being filled with the Spirit's power the disciples will be prepared to be witnesses for Christ's kingdom from Jerusalem to the ends of the earth.

The first two chapters of Acts convey the meaning that the work of Christ's kingdom will go forward through the empowering of the Spirit. The work of Christ and the work of the Spirit, therefore, are not two different works. Christ and the Spirit do the *one* work of the kingdom. The Spirit is the earthly continuation of Jesus' proclamation of the kingdom. This fact stands in direct opposition to the Pentecostal claim that the Spirit does a different work from that of Christ.

In Acts 1:4-5 Jesus makes the promise of the Spirit to the disciples. Jesus' promise also upsets Pentecostal categories. You will remember that in Pentecostal theology the reception of the Spirit comes on those who have met the conditions, totally yielded themselves, had complete faith and done all the *more's* required of them. Nothing like that is in evidence in this passage.

Jesus calls the Spirit the promise of the Father. The Father gives the Spirit to men because he has promised to do so, not because men have somehow deserved it. To receive the Spirit, Jesus simply tells the disciples to *wait* in Jerusalem. There are no conditions here. There isn't anything that they should *do*. They just wait. Waiting is the only way to receive a promise. Jesus announces that those who wait shall be baptized with the Holy Spirit. They *shall be* baptized. That's a fact. That's the promise. *All* the disciples will receive the promise of the Father. Again, no conditions are laid down. It doesn't say that only those who are worthy will receive the Spirit. It doesn't say that only those who have total faith and obedience will receive the Spirit. "You shall be baptized with the Holy Spirit." That's what it says.

The book of Acts is consistent at this point. Throughout

the narrative the Spirit's coming to men is always based on the Father's promise. Those who receive the Spirit are not active seekers but passive receivers. They wait and the Spirit comes. He comes to all who wait and trust the promise. No conditions. Just wait. The Spirit moves toward waiting men. It isn't that men move towards the Spirit who waits for them in order to baptize them.

Looking further down the corridors of Acts we must pay some attention to the four passages which speak of the coming of the Spirit, the gift of tongues, baptism and the laying on of hands (Acts 2:1-42; 8:14-17; 10:1–11:18; 19:1-7). The order of events in these passages is not consistent and, therefore, problematic. (See chart.) In Acts

### THE COMING OF THE SPIRIT IN ACTS

**Acts 2:1-4**
a) wind blows
b) tongues of fire
c) filled with Spirit
d) tongues

**Acts 2:37-38**
a) call to repent
b) Christian baptism
c) receive Spirit

**Acts 8:14-17**
a) baptism in name of Jesus
b) laying on of hands
c) receive Spirit

**Acts 10:1—11:18**
a) Peter's sermon
b) receive Spirit
c) tongues
d) Christian baptism

**Acts 19:1-7**
a) John's baptism
b) Jesus' baptism
c) laying on of hands
d) receive Spirit
e) tongues

2:1-4, a) the wind (remember the Old Testament use of the words wind, breath, Spirit) comes from heaven, b)

tongues of fire rest on the disciples, c) they were all filled
with the Spirit and d) began to speak in other tongues.
At the end of Acts 2 (vv. 37-38) the order is a) a call to
repentance, b) baptism and the c) reception of the gift of
the Holy Spirit by all who are baptized. In Acts 8 there
is a) baptism in the name of the Lord Jesus, b) the laying
on of hands and c) the reception of the Holy Spirit. In
Acts 10 and 11 a) Peter's preaching of the Word is accompanied by b) the outpouring of the Holy Spirit on the
Gentiles. The evidence of this outpouring is c) glossolalia
which becomes the just cause for d) baptizing Gentiles
into the Christian faith. In Acts 19 the order of things is
a) baptism into John's baptism, b) baptism in the name
of the Lord Jesus, c) the laying on of hands, d) the reception of the Holy Spirit and e) glossolalia.

The contradictions between these passages are obvious.
We cannot be satisfied to place a priority on those passages
we like and to neglect those that are more difficult for
our position. Four conclusions can be drawn from these
passages.

1. It is impossible to make the details of these passages
agree with one another. Acts presents no consistent theology of the relationship between baptism, the Holy Spirit,
laying on of hands and glossolalia. Luke tells four stories.
The details of those stories do not correspond. We must
be careful not to find symmetry and meaning where there
is none.

2. The coming of the Spirit is never disassociated from
the proclamation of the work of Jesus. The disciples, of
course, knew Jesus' work from firsthand experience. In
each of the other instances the proclamation of Jesus seems
to be the prerequisite for the coming of the Spirit. On the

day of Pentecost it was after Peter's sermon that repentance, baptism, and the gift of the Spirit happened. It was during Peter's preaching that the Spirit fell on Cornelius and the Gentiles. The Spirit is given where the name of Jesus is proclaimed. That seems to be the fact of the matter. The work of Jesus and the work of the Spirit are seen in the closest possible relationship.

3. The first Pentecost is a unique experience. It is not the pattern for the other stories in Acts where the Spirit is given. It is an exception to the pattern. The pattern in the remaining events is that Christian baptism with water stands in an integral relationship to the giving of the Spirit. In Acts 2:37-38 those who are baptized receive the Holy Spirit. In Acts 8 those who had been baptized in the name of the Lord Jesus received the laying on of hands in order to receive the Spirit. In Acts 10 those who receive the Spirit (evidenced through speaking in tongues) are immediately baptized. In Acts 19 those who were baptized into John's baptism of repentance are re-baptized in the name of the Lord Jesus thus receiving the Holy Spirit.

The details of these passages vary. What is unmistakably clear, however, is that *after Pentecost the Holy Spirit is never separated from water baptism*. Water baptism and Spirit baptism are not two separate events. The giving of the Spirit stands in the closest possible relationship to baptism with water. To be baptized with Christian baptism (water and the Word) is to receive the gift of the Holy Spirit.

4. The fourth conclusion is a very important one and will require greater elaboration. As indicated, these four passages cannot be harmonized in their details.

Among the many purposes that could be advanced for

the book of Acts, Luke's own purpose stands out clearly at the beginning of his work. The *purpose* and *outline* of Acts can be found in Acts 1:8: "But you shall receive power when the Holy Spirit has come upon you; and you shall be my witnesses in Jerusalem and in all Judea and Samaria and to the end of the earth." This purpose and the passages which carry out the purpose can be diagrammed as follows:

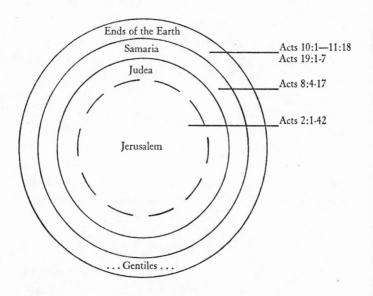

Luke's testimony to the work of the Spirit is not a testimony concerning the work of the Spirit in the lives of individuals. His testimony to the Spirit concerns the Spirit's *corporate* work. He is concerned with the work of the Spirit as the power that enabled the church to move out geographically from Jerusalem to Judea (the "state" in which Jerusalem was located) to the neighboring "state" of Samaria and on even into the world of the Gentiles, to the ends of the earth. That's where the Spirit was leading the church.

In order to portray this moving out of the church under the Spirit's power, Luke tells a series of Pentecostal and *mini-Pentecostal* stories. The first story is that of Pentecost in Jerusalem. That's where the spread of the church begins.

The next Pentecostal explosioin takes place in Samaria. That's the story told in Acts 8. To appreciate the meaning of this story we must remember that there was a bitter hatred between Jews (the early Christians were all Jews) and Samaritans. Remember what the Samaritan woman said to Jesus? "How is it that you, a Jew, ask a drink of me, a woman of Samaria?" John, the gospel writer, added his own comment to her statement. "For Jews have no dealings with Samaritans" (John 4:9).

This background enables us to capture the central significance of the Acts 8 passage. Apostles from Jerusalem go down to Samaria to lay hands on the Samaritan Christians! Through this laying on of hands the Samaritans received the Holy Spirit. (Glossolalia is not mentioned in this story.) The Spirit had pushed the church from Jerusalem to Samaria. The Spirit enables the church to grow by breaking down the barriers between people. In Acts 2 the Spirit broke a language barrier enabling Jews from every nation to hear the mighty works of God in their own tongue!

Acts 10:1–11:18 is the most carefully-told Pentecostal story in the entire book of Acts. The Spirit is on the brink of pushing the church across another barrier. Gentiles will be embraced in Christ's fellowship as well as Jews. Jews and Gentiles had practically nothing to do with each other. To expect a good Jew like Peter to go to the Gentiles was a real "Mission Impossible." But God got the job done. It took a vision and some real pushing but Peter did go to the house of the Gentile centurion, Cornelius. He preached to him concerning the forgiveness of sins in the name of Jesus. While he was preaching the Spirit fell on all who heard the gospel and they began to speak in tongues. Peter had no choice now. He had to baptize them and include them in the church's fellowship.

When Peter went back to Jerusalem he was criticized for baptizing Gentiles. Had Peter gone mad? Peter rose to his defense. "I had to baptize them," he said. "It was just like Pentecost all over again." "As I began to speak, the Holy Spirit fell on them just as on us at the beginning" (Acts 11:15). Just like the beginning. Just like Pentecost! Luke clearly tells this story as a Gentile Pentecost.

Once Peter and his Jerusalem friends became convinced that Gentiles could receive the Spirit too, they glorified God. They did not, however, glory in the fact that Gentiles spoke in tongues. They gloried because "to the Gentiles also God has granted repentance unto life" (Acts 11:18).

Luke's final "Pentecost" story takes place in Ephesus (Acts 19). Ephesus is almost the end of the earth when you start from Jerusalem. The Spirit manifests himself in a far-off land. His mission is reaching its purpose. He has enabled the church to move out and grow. He has broken down one barrier after another as he draws men and nations together in the fellowship of Christ.

That is the "big picture" of the Spirit's work in Acts. It's a corporate work, a work of church growth and new possibilities of fellowship. We should not get side-tracked by differences in individual passages. We need to catch the view of his grand landscape: Jerusalem, Samaria, and the ends of the earth! This picture must always be kept in mind when we ask about the meaning of glossolalia in particular and the work of the Holy Spirit in general in the book of Acts. Glossolalia in Acts is one of the signs of the Spirit's moving power in the growth of the church to the ends of the earth. That is the unity of all of the seeming disunity about this gift in Luke's account. Any study of Acts which derives a meaning for glossolalia from individual passages alone failing to see the function of this gift of the Spirit in the overall thrust of Luke's work misses the important point!

Many Christians will still have some problems with the book of Acts. Acts does not present a good foundation for building a theology of spiritual experience. It is not a good biblical foundation for neo-Pentecostalism. Luke's description of the work of the Spirit often seems to be more akin to the Old Testament understanding of the work of the Spirit than it is to the understanding of the Spirit as described in John and Paul. Three examples illustrate this.

a) Luke has a tendency (probably because of the needs of his readers) to see the Spirit as the immediate solution to any human problem. The Spirit is always working things out in Acts. Every story has a happy ending for the "good guys." Paul, especially in the Corinthian correspondence, is much more realistic about life in the Spirit.

b) Luke can sometimes separate salvation from the work of the Spirit. Acts 8 is a good example of this. In the Old Testament the work of the Spirit was not necessarily associated with salvation either. For Paul, however, the declaration that "Jesus is Lord" on the part of the Christian is the fundamental evidence of the Spirit's work.

c) Luke prefers to point to spectacular and extraordinary signs as the evidence of the Spirit's presence. Glossolalia is one example. One can think here of the spectacular works done by the "charismatic" judges in the Old Testament. Paul's lists of charismatic gifts, on the other hand, include both ordinary (administration, teaching, stewardship) and extraordinary gifts.

Luke's total presentation of the work of the Spirit, however, is very close to that of Paul and contains some important and sometimes neglected elements. He describes the work of the Spirit as a corporate work. The Spirit enables the church to grow and come together. The Spirit's work is a work of gathering individuals into an ever-wider fellowship. The Spirit breaks down the barriers that separate us from each other. The result of this work of the Spirit is the world-wide fellowship of the Christian church. What the Spirit does to us as individuals is a step on the way to his work of incorporating us into the body of Christ. The church is the work and the workshop of the Holy Spirit. It is through the work of that church in which we are baptized in the name of Jesus that we, too, might receive the gift of the Spirit of God.

# 8

# We Walk by Faith, Not by Sight

*Now faith is the assurance of things hoped for, the
conviction of things not seen (Heb. 11:1).
We walk by faith, not by sight (2 Cor. 5:7).*

Thomas was the original doubter. His Lord had been
crucified. His world had been shattered. He was absent
when the resurrected Christ appeared to the disciples
breathing on them and granting them the Holy Spirit
(John 20:19-23). Can you imagine how excited the disciples were when they finally found Thomas and could
tell him the good news! "We have seen the Lord" (John
20:25). "Can you believe it, Thomas? We have seen him
with our own eyes. He's not dead. He lives."

"I don't believe it." That was Thomas' reply to the good
news. "Unless I see in his hands the print of the nails, and
place my finger in the mark of the nails, and place my
hand in his side, I will not believe" (John 20:25). "I've got
to see it to believe it."

Eight days later he saw it. Jesus came to the disciples

again. He went directly to doubting Thomas. He didn't scold him. No harsh words. "Put your finger here, and see my hands; and put out your hand, and place it in my side; do not be faithless, but believing" (John 20:27). Thomas believed. *Now* he believed. Seeing, he could believe it. Jesus then spoke a word to Thomas which was clearly directed down the long corridors of history. Not many more were going to be able to see in order to believe. Thomas was an exception. "Have you believed because you have seen me? Blessed are those who have not seen and yet believe" (John 20:29). Thomas wanted to walk by sight in order to have faith. Jesus made it quite clear that faith is not normally caused by seeing. Thomas believed *because* he saw. Most of us believe *in spite of* the fact that we have not seen what Thomas nor the disciples saw.

In many instances the neo-Pentecostal movement is filled not with doubting Thomases but with *believing* Thomases. They have turned the story of Thomas around. Thomas wouldn't believe unless he saw. Many today claim that *we will see if we believe*. For Thomas, sight brought faith. For many today, faith brings sight.

Surprisingly, Jesus' words apply with equal force to doubting and believing Thomases. Jesus' word to Thomas cut the nerve cord between faith and sight. Seeing should not be a requirement for believing. Believing should not be a requirement for seeing. The passages quoted at the outset of this chapter also sever the link between faith and sight. The author of Hebrews understands faith precisely as a hope for that which is *unseen*. St. Paul claimed that Christians walk by faith and not by sight.

These passages are a warning alarm to all within the

Christian community who wish to re-establish the connection between faith and sight. Let us discuss two areas in which this connection comes close to re-establishment: guidance and healing. The spiritual upsurge connected with Pentecostalism and neo-Pentecostalism has brought these areas to the attention and practice of many people. Each holds out the tempting offer that we can live by sight through our faith. When that happens, when faith produces sight, there is a danger of turning the New Testament witness to the relationship between faith and sight upside down.

## Guidance

The question of guidance is in close relationship to the interpretation of tongues and prophecy. We have talked about the necessity of interpreting that which is publicly spoken in tongues. We have also maintained that the content of prophecy is not to be distinguished from the content of an interpretation. A prophecy is a word spoken in plain language without a preceding tongue; interpretation is a word spoken in ordinary speech that follows or interprets what has been spoken in tongues.

The content of interpretations and prophecies varies. Sometimes God is praised. Sometimes words which proclaim the nature and activity of God are given. Sometimes those hearing the interpretation are admonished. Sometimes there are words which must be considered guidance. Directions are given. Specific instructions are set forth. Events which might happen in the future (next year or tomorrow) are spoken of. Guidance is an integral part of prophecy and interpretation for most neo-Pentecostals.

I have personally experienced guidance on a number of occasions.

The most outstanding case of such guidance took place at one of the crossroads in my life. As we are often inclined to do, I was concerned with my future. What should I be doing? How and where should I serve God? Actually, I wasn't the only one involved. A number of us were covenanted in prayer together for many days, wrestling with the question of the future. We were sure God would answer us with a clear and guiding word. Nothing came. We prayed some more. We waited. Then it happened. An experience we shall never forget. We were on a lakeshore and the hour was late. Our sons came bursting into the room. "Come quick. Look at the sky. Look at the stars." The children were aflame with excitement. They sensed something mystifying at hand. One had even thought of singing "We three kings" as the accompaniment for the announcement!

What we saw were two very bright stars reflecting across the water. They met each other in a gigantic V at the very point of our lake front. We wondered if God might be calling us to work in a place located directly out from the point of that V-shape. Specific guidance confirmed that speculation. The stars were God's signs. They pointed the direction of our future. The words of guidance we received spelled things out in some detail. As the months went by this guidance to a most unlikely task and a most unlikely opportunity unraveled itself step by step. It happened almost exactly the way our guidance had indicated.

Other examples could be given. Most neo-Pentecostals have such experiences. But what is the meaning of such guidance? Does it mean that if we have enough faith God will give us guidance (sight) for every step of life's way? Is guidance a way through faith to walk by sight? This would most certainly be a Spirit-led life! Literally Spirit-led. Each step announced beforehand. Everything laid out precisely. Surely that is the way it should be. We are tempted to believe that the only thing that holds any of us back from such Spirit-leading is our lack of faith. If we had enough faith, we could all walk by sight.

Such is the temptation of guidance. It tempts us to walk by sight and not by faith. It tempts us to feel guilty over a lack of faith if we don't come to sight. The message is always the same: *If we had faith, we could be Spirit-led.* I call it a temptation because that's what it is. It is a temptation to live beyond faith.

I have been very interested in what others have written about guidance. Over the years I have formed certain opinions on the matter. Fortunately those opinions have been confirmed by others writing on the same subject. One author, for example, indicated that from 60 to 70 percent of the personal guidances he had received proved to be wrong. I don't know what the percentages are but I, too, have experienced guidance which proved to be false. Some writers conclude that guidance should be *confirmational rather than directional.* That is a helpful distinction. Guidance may be used as confirmation of a direction; it should not provide the direction by itself.

In his section on "spiritual gifts" in 1 Corinthians Paul has two words that apply at this point. In 1 Corinthians 13:9 he says, ". . . our prophecy is imperfect." In 14:32 he counsels that the ". . . spirits of prophets are subject to prophets." Prophecy, including guidance, is imperfect. It should never, therefore, be trusted as the *sole criterion* for a future action. The rest of the prophets (the fellowship of the church) should be consulted. Many questions should be asked. Does this guidance stand in agreement with Holy Scripture? Does the community agree? Does common sense (God gives us that gift too!) support it? Do the circumstances bear it out? These and many other questions are legitimate tests of any guidance. A word of guidance, in and of itself, should not be sufficient grounds for action. (People have actually been swindled out of large sums of money because someone "guided by the Spirit" told them to give them their funds!)

Guidance, in other words, is not sufficient grounds in and of itself to move from faith to sight. Guidance must be tested. Our brothers and sisters in the faith (including those who have given us the Bible and our theologies) should help us test the spirits.

When Christians make decisions we make them within the context of several boundaries. Our decisions are bounded on the one hand by Holy Scripture. They are bounded further by the wise counsel of the community, our own ability to think, common sense, guidance and so on. Boundaried by these factors and limitations we make decisions. Sometimes a single factor will dominate our decision. At other times several factors will be taken into account. In any case we make our decision out of faith and not out of sight. We don't know what the outcome will be; we trust the hands of God.

One of Luther's associates, Philip Melanchthon, had a decision to make. He didn't know what to do. He wanted to do the right thing. The right thing is the sight thing! That's what he evidently was thinking. He couldn't *see* for sure what he should do. Not being able to see, he was unable to act. Luther told him to act without seeing. "Sin boldly, and believe in Christ all the more boldly still." That was Luther's famous advice. He wasn't counselling his friend to sin. He was urging him to make a decision and leave the results of that action in the forgiving hands of God. That's exactly what it means to walk by faith and not by sight. We often walk blindly into the future trusting that God will uphold us and forgive us, even if some of our decisions and actions are poorly chosen.

Guidance by the Spirit can certainly be one of the boundaries of Christian decision making. We must not, however, understand guidance as the way men and women of "true" faith walk by sight. To claim to walk by sight rather than faith is to claim to walk a path beyond that promised by Jesus and the New Testament.

## Healing

The Pentecostal churches have brought renewed attention to the ministry of healing. The Pentecostal view of church history divides that history into two phases. 1) The Early Rain. In the days of the early church the Spirit worked mightily among his people. Evidence of this work can be seen in the many miracles, including healing, that took place. The miraculous soon faded from view, however. This was evidence that the Spirit was no longer as mightily at work among his people.

2) The Latter Rain. With the bursting forth of Pentecostalism the Spirit and his miracles returned. The 20th century is clearly an age of the Spirit. It is an age like that early age. The church today, at least in its Pentecostal form, looks like the church described in the book of Acts. Acts,

as we have said earlier, is to be the pattern and obligatory model for church life today, according to Pentecostal thinking. There was healing then; there should be healing today.

Americans have been aware of this Pentecostal healing ministry whether or not they were able to identify its roots. Oral Roberts, for example, began his Christian ministry as a Pentecostal "faith healer." Many of the other radio and TV personalities who have carried on a ministry of healing are also Pentecostals.

The underlying theological premise of the Pentecostal churches with respect to healing has been: *Anyone who believes is healed; anyone who is not healed has not believed aright.* Such theology is accurately described by the words: *faith healing.* If you have faith, you will get well. If you don't, you won't. It's that simple. We have again an instance of faith that leads to sight. If you believe, truly believe, really believe, you will *see* the results of your believing. If you are sick, you will see health. Faith leads to sight.

In many instances, neo-Pentecostals have been influenced by this Pentecostal view of divine or faith healing. As we indicated earlier, neo-Pentecostals, having little theological framework for interpreting their experiences, found a ready-made framework of interpretation in Pentecostal theology. This may have happened unconsciously more than consciously but it happened nevertheless. Many neo-Pentecostals, who have been involved in healing ministries, appear to hold a premise identical to that of their theological mentors: "Anyone who believes is healed; anyone who is not healed has not believed aright."

What shall we say about healing? It seems at times that we are locked between extreme positions. On the one hand the Pentecostals and others maintain that "true" faith will bring healing. On the other hand, theologians under the influence of scientific Western mentality have often separated healing completely from the context of the Christian faith. You go to the doctor if you're sick. You can go to Jesus with your sins.

Personally, I cannot accept either of these positions. To proclaim, as the Pentecostals do, that faith always brings healing is to make more of faith than the Bible does. Faith becomes man's work. It is our response to God. If we have enough of it we can conquer all obstacles. If we have enough faith we can walk by sight. Faith leads to sight. In this system faith becomes the *human* key which makes God respond to man. If we have the right kind of faith, God is programmed to respond in set and certain ways. God becomes the idol that we manipulate rather than the sovereign Lord of our lives.

The Pentecostal view of faith in reference to healing is also problematic in the way in which it creates guilt. We will be healed *if* we have faith. *If* we aren't healed the problem is clear. Our faith is weak, insufficient, and infantile. *If* we aren't healed it's our own fault. We must look within ourselves for the problem. What's the matter with our faith? Where have we gone wrong? How can we do better? Those kinds of questions produce guilt. The gospel promises freedom from guilt. Faith is trust in the forgiving word of the gospel. Faith always lives out of God's love. When faith is turned around in such a way that trying to "get it" produces guilt then that understanding of faith is on a collision course with the New Testament.

Paul had just this problem with the Christians in Galatia. They believed in faith as a kind of first step. After that they advised Christians to do all kinds of "spiritual" works of the law (call it yielding, surrender, total obedience or whatever) in order to increase faith. Paul told them that *faith begins and ends with hearing*. Hearing the gospel creates faith. Doing, any doing that we do, does not make faith more faithful. It can even destroy faith. It becomes something other than faith. Here's how Paul puts it:

> Did you receive the Spirit by works of the law, or by hearing with faith? Are you so foolish? Having begun with the Spirit [hearing], are you now ending with the flesh [doing]? (Gal. 3:2-3).

Faith lives only and forever out of the hearing of God's good word of forgiveness. Faith can never be man's tool for guaranteeing that God will re-act to him in a certain way. God creates faith. Faith doesn't create God's response.

The point should be clear. It is difficult to accept the view that says: "Anyone who believes is healed." But it is just as difficult to accept the nearly total neglect of the ministry of healing in most churches today. That equally denies and distorts the New Testament witness. Jesus didn't just forgive sins. He healed people of their diseases.

Modern psychology has reminded us that mind and body are integrally related to each other (psychosomatic). A sick mind can produce a sick body. A sick body can produce a sick mind. Jesus knew that. The Greek word used for the salvation brought by Jesus means *health*. Jesus offered wholeness for mind and body. To talk about the gospel of salvation and not talk about health, physical health, forces us to cut out about one-third of the gospel narratives. Health is part of the gospel. We can't just run away from that fact. We can't just say, "Well, that was fine for them to believe that in the first century. Today we know better."

What we do know better today is the art of medical

science. Scientists are constantly discovering new cures for old ailments. Thank God for them. Thank God for modern medicine! In any discussion about healing we must recognize that *all healing comes from God.* I sometimes hear a distinction made between "natural" and "supernatural" healing. We have all heard of cases where people only trusted "supernatural" healing and refused the help that was available through natural, medical channels. The result of such misplaced trust has sometimes been disastrous.

The distinction between natural and supernatural healing is a false distinction. Nature, after all, is God's handiwork. God gave us the authority and the commission to be the stewards of his handiwork. When we exercise that stewardship with our God given brains to discover *miracle* drugs we are simply acting as good stewards of the Creator's earth. In other words, what is often looked down on as "only natural" healing is every bit as much God's work as that healing which some call "supernatural." All healing comes from God. Healing comes from God our Creator and from God our Redeemer. That is the *only distinction* we should make with regard to healing. In either case it is the one God who is the author of all healing.

In order to discuss the healing power of God the Redeemer we need to avoid the pitfalls we have mentioned. The healing power of the gospel should not be understood as *dependent* on our faith nor should our understanding of the Christian faith omit the possibility of the healing power of God the Redeemer. The best course of action with reference to "redemptive" healing is to relate our prayers for health to the word and sacraments of the church. This is most easily done in connection with the Lord's Supper.

The Lord's Supper has many meanings. As a visible and
public sign of the presence of Christ's gospel one of its
meanings is that it is a place of salvation, a place of health.
The Lord's Supper could easily be understood as the
church's primary healing service.

Several opportunities have been given to me to minister
to people in ill health who have asked for prayers for healing. My procedure has usually been as follows. Get a community of Christian friends to be present. Explain that
the sick person has asked for prayers for healing. In our
prayers we should understand that God's ultimate will is
the health of his children. God's will *is* that we be whole!
We know he will win the final battle over sickness and
death in the hour of resurrection. In this life we experience
the first fruits of that victory. God certainly has the power
to heal our diseases whenever he wishes. We pray, therefore, that the healing power of God break forth from the
future into the present life of this sick one. We are to pray
*expecting* health to happen.

After we have prayed expectantly, the Lord's Supper is
administered to the community present. The bread and
wine are the vehicles of God's redemptive and healing
presence. If healing is to happen it can happen as the Spirit
uses the elements of bread and wine to create health. Health
does not come through the faith of the one in charge of
the service. Health does not come if the sick person believes
aright. Health comes when the Spirit creates in our midst
today, through material things like bread and wine, the
first fruits of his final healing work.

Sometimes such a ministry has resulted in the healing
of the sick person. Other times it has not. There is no set
formula. God's time is not our time. The faith that we

bring to a prayer for healing is that God knows what he is about with our lives and our health. Faith prays expectantly for healing and leaves the results confidently in the hands of God. If our prayers are not answered in the way we prayed and willed, our faith looks to God in the confidence that he is in control of the situation. Unfaith looks instead at the self or the sick person and questions the amount of "true" faith that accompanied the prayer. "Anyone who is not healed has not believed aright." Such an attitude is the greatest unfaith of all! It trusts human faith more than it trusts God. Unfaith refuses to let God be God.

Redemptive healing is possible. It does happen. It does not, however, depend on us. Healing is God's to give. We can *expect* him to give that gift to us. But we don't *know* that he will. We never know. We never control God. Truly, we walk by faith, not by sight.

# 9

# The Gifts of the Spirit
# and the Cross of Christ

*I think that I am not in the least inferior to these superlative apostles (2 Cor. 11:5).*
*Three times I besought the Lord about this (thorn) in the flesh) that it should leave me; but he said to me, "My grace is sufficient for you, for my power is made perfect in weakness." I will all the more gladly boast of my weaknesses, that the power of Christ may rest upon me (2 Cor. 12:8-9).*

The call by many Christians today to live through faith to sight is not a new one. It's at least as old as the New Testament. It's exactly what many of the Corinthian Christians believed. (Paul's admonition that we walk by faith and not by sight was addressed to the Corinthian Christians: 2 Cor. 5:7.) What we are witnessing today in many quarters, therefore, is a revival of the Corinthian heresy, the heresy that claims that Christians live by sight. The Corinthians were critical of any Christians who did not *see*. They were critical of Paul on that account. He didn't seem to measure up to their exalted standards.

Paul's letters to the Corinthians are very important for us today, therefore, in at least two aspects.

1. They help us frame an answer to those who might accuse us of lack of faith. Such accusations, unfortunately, have been associated with some aspects of neo-Pentecostalism. A kind of spiritual judgmentalism sets in. Those who "have the Spirit" criticize those who don't measure up to their standards and who obviously lack spiritual openness and attunedness. If we had their kind of faith, the argument runs, we would also have their kind of spirituality. How do we answer such "spiritual accusers?" Paul shows us the way in his defense of his own spirituality and apostleship to the super-Christians at Corinth.

2. These letters help us understand the meaning and place of spiritual gifts more than any other passages in the New Testament. Speaking in tongues, for example, is only mentioned in two New Testament books: Acts and 1 Corinthians. (A third mention is made in the later ending to the book of Mark: 16:9-20.) Acts tells a story about the Spirit's role, including the gift of tongues, in the growth and cohesion of the early church. As we have seen, Pentecostals and many neo-Pentecostals build their understanding of the gift of tongues primarily upon these passages. The argument here is that 1 Corinthians is a much better basis for understanding the nature of spiritual gifts than is the book of Acts. In 1 Corinthians 12–14 Paul attempts to interpret the meaning of spiritual gifts for those who had misunderstood them. His insights provide us with the New Testament's most helpful clues for understanding spiritual gifts.

## Superlative Apostles

In order to understand Paul's arguments in his Corinthian letters, we must understand the nature of the people he is addressing. We'll call them super-Christians. At least that is what they thought they were. In the passage quoted above Paul refers to them as "superlative apostles." Who were these super-Christians? What did these superlative apostles believe?

We can begin with a simple answer. They believed in *Christ*. The super-Christians were probably the "Christ party" that is mentioned in the Corinthian correspondence (see 1 Cor. 1:12; 2 Cor. 10:7 and 11:12-14 for examples). They belonged to Christ. Not to Jesus! To Christ. In their minds Jesus was the name of a man who was for and from the earth. To be earthly was to be unspiritual. It has been suggested that the super-Christians even cursed the earthly Jesus (1 Cor. 12:3). Why curse the earthly Jesus? In order to show that one's allegiance is not to a man of earth but to a God from heaven. Jesus rose from the dead and became the Messiah, the Christ. The Corinthians seem to have understood Christ as the heavenly, spiritual man while Jesus was understood as the earthly, physical man. The Corinthian super-Christians were interested in the spiritual (Christ), not the earthly (Jesus).

The spiritual "Christ party" in Corinth claimed, therefore, to live spiritually with Christ in his resurrection. They lived beyond the earth. They lived beyond Jesus. They lived beyond the problems of this life (cross). They lived by sight (beyond faith).

If this is an accurate portrayal of the super-Christian Corinthian spiritualists it may explain a number of passages in the Corinthian correspondence. It may explain, for example, why they thought they lived above and beyond the law. Laws are mere earthly regulations. They don't apply to spiritual people! "All things are lawful for me" (1 Cor. 6:12). That's what they told Paul. Living above the law therefore "freed" them to commit incest (1 Cor. 5). Being "spiritual" meant also that they were knowledgeable, "all of us possess knowledge" (1 Cor. 8:1). They told Paul that, too. With their superior brand of knowledge they could eat meat that had been offered to idols even though other Christians were quite upset by their actions.

The fact that they believed that they lived with Christ, beyond the cares and laws and customs of this earth, may also explain why they didn't believe in the resurrection. In 1 Corinthians 15 Paul argues in detail and at length that there shall be a resurrection from the dead at the end of time. The superlative apostles evidently thought that they had *already been raised* with Christ. For them resurrection was not a future hope. It was a present reality. They lived with Christ now. The problems of earth were behind them. Anyone who still suffered with common, earthly problems simply wasn't as spiritual as they were.

When one lived with Christ in the world of the spiritual then spiritual manifestations were in evidence. That's how you could tell super-Christians from ordinary Christians. They received the gifts of the Spirit. Superlative apostles spoke in tongues. They performed miracles. They had great faith. They were wise. The list was impressive. Spiritual people evidence spiritual gifts. That's just the way it was. So you could tell (the super-Christians could certainly tell!) who were "Christ's party" and who were not.

That may well be why they ate the Lord's Supper only with the "in" group. That way everyone could see who the genuine Christians were (see 1 Cor. 11:18-19).

Super-Christians thought they were in a good position to judge and criticize the not-so-super, earth-bound Christians. They were always judging. They even judged Paul. It was obvious to the super-Christians, for example, that Paul wasn't one of them. Paul still had problems connected with the "unspiritual" world. He had that thorn in the flesh. A super-Christian wouldn't have that! Furthermore, Paul wasn't much to look at or listen to. He spoke with much fear and trembling. Paul may have been a Christian. In their minds, however, he certainly was not a super-Christian.

## The Foolishness of the Cross

How was Paul to answer his spiritual "superiors?" He does answer them in the Corinthian letters. What he said to them is very important. You can use it almost word for word the next time a super-Christian looks down at you. In 1 Corinthians 1 that answer begins to take shape. The Corinthians claimed to live with Christ in a spiritual world beyond the resurrection. They evidently viewed the cross as a mere introduction to resurrection life. Not so, said Paul. The cross is not so easily left behind. In fact *it is the cross, not the resurrection, which marks the life of the Christian.* Christian proclamation is a proclamation of the cross.

Super-Christians of all ages proclaim a Christian faith that lives under the banner of resurrection glory. They maintain that the marks of resurrection should be manifest in the lives of God's people. Those marks always bear the character of triumph, victory, glory and miracle.

Christianity lived under the banner of the cross does not appear so mighty and glorious. That's what Paul told the Corinthians. That's his reminder to Christians in all ages who fix their attention upon the resurrection and the glory of being a Christian, thus tending to forget the cross. The cross is the symbol that *God's triumph appears under the form of its opposite*. The cross looks like defeat; it's really God's place of victory. The cross looks like death but it is life. It looks like the end; it's only the beginning.

The cross turns all of our conventional wisdom upside down. It baffles us. God's Son on a cross? A cross as God's throne of victory? Who can understand that? Who can make sense out of it?

> Where is the wise man? Where is the scribe? Where is the debater of this age? Has not God made foolish the wisdom of the world? For since, in the wisdom of God, the world did not know God through wisdom, it pleased God through the folly of what we preach to save those who believe. For Jews demand signs and Greeks seek wisdom, but we preach Christ crucified, a stumbling block to Jews and folly to Gentiles, but to those who are called, both Jews and Greeks, Christ the power of God and the wisdom of God. For the foolishness of God is wiser than men, and the weakness of God is stronger than men.

> For consider your call, brethren; not many of you were wise according to worldly standards, not many were powerful, not many were of noble birth; but God chose what is foolish in the world to shame the wise, God chose what is weak in the world to shame the strong, God chose what is low and despised in the world, even things that are not, to bring to nothing things that are, so that no human being might boast in the presence of God (1 Cor. 1:20-29).

There it is! Paul's theology of the cross. It's a bewildering proclamation. A crucified carpenter's son is God's salvation! Sinners are called saints. The lowliest things in the world become the greatest. God makes that happen. He does it that way in order that "no human being might boast in the presence of God." The cross puts an end to boasting. Super-Christians who live beyond the cross under the banner of resurrection glory love to boast of the signs of their "Christianness." The Corinthian super-Christians boasted of spiritual gifts. They boasted of miraculous signs in their lives. They boasted about living above and beyond sin and the law.

Paul, in effect, said to them: "You've got it backwards. If you want to boast you ought to boast of the things that show your weakness and foolishness." (Paul's main argument of defense along these lines can be found in 2 Cor. 10–12.) "If I must boast, I will boast of the things that show my weakness" (2 Cor. 11:30). Paul boasts, therefore, of the thorn in his flesh. Super-Christians said that a "true" Christian wouldn't have such a thorn. Paul replied by saying that *thorns are precisely the mark of a Christian.* We are weak, thorn-marked, helpless people. What, then, is our hope? Our hope is that thorns are also the sign of God's strength and grace. "My grace is sufficient for you, for my power is made perfect in weakness" (2 Cor. 12:9). That's what God told Paul. "My son was broken on a cross. You are broken by many a thorn. Though the world can't understand it, I call crosses thrones. I call thorn-plagued-people saints. My grace is sufficient for you."

In 1 Corinthians 15:25-28 Paul reminds the superlative apostles that our earthly problems are not over. Death is the last enemy and death has not yet been conquered.

Furthermore he tells them that the reign of the Christ they adore will come to an end. He, too, must finally be subjected to God so that God may be all in all.

That's the shape of Paul's answer to his super-Christian critics. "Paul," they said, "how can you call yourself a Christian when you have so many earthly problems?" "Super-Christians," said Paul, "the cross means that God loves people with earthly problems. My earthly problems force me to live by grace alone. My thorns constantly remind me that God works in the midst of my weakness. My thorns and weaknesses and hardships are the proof of my apostleship!" (See also 1 Cor. 4:8-13; 2 Cor. 6:1-10.)

A word needs to be said here concerning 1 Corinthians 3:1. This passage is used by Watchman Nee and others to show that there are two kinds of Christians: spiritual and carnal (fleshly). The point, of course, is that we should strive to be spiritual and not carnal Christians.

Such an interpretation of this passage makes it say almost the opposite of what Paul meant. Remember whom he was addressing? He was speaking to so-called super-Christians. He was addressing Christians who certainly considered themselves to be spiritual. Paul, however, doesn't call them spiritual at all. He doesn't refer to them as super-Christians. He calls them babies! "But I, brethren, could not address you as spiritual men, but as men of the flesh, as babes in Christ." Is it any wonder that the Corinthians didn't like Paul. Super-Christians would surely like to forget that these letters were ever written.

## Charismata and the Cross

Let's turn our attention to 1 Corinthians 12–14 where Paul discusses the matter of spiritual gifts. We've seen the context of those chapters. Some of the Corinthian Christians claimed to live out their Christian life beyond the cross in the power and glory and miracle of the resurrection. They lived spiritually with the resurrected Christ. One of the *proofs* of their spiritual elevation over matters of the earth was that they possessed gifts relating to the world of the spiritual. That was how they interpreted the meaning of spiritual gifts. Spiritual gifts were the sign of spiritual, super-Christians.

As we have seen, Paul does not accept that viewpoint. Paul calls the Corinthian Christians to come down from the resurrection to the cross. He calls them to come down from the spiritual world to the earth. He calls them to remember Jesus as well as Christ.

Paul offered his own definition of spiritual life. To be spiritual does not mean to live *beyond* this world and its problems. To be spiritual is to live *in* this world, in the midst of thorns and brokenness, confident of the final victory. Spiritual gifts, therefore, are not signs that one has overcome the world. They are not signs that one has moved *beyond* the world. Spiritual gifts are to be used *in* the world. They are given for *earthly* service, not *heavenly* glory. They are given for the common good. (See Chapter Two.) They are given for the edification and upbuilding of the body of Christ.

Paul knows that Christians possess different spiritual gifts as they live out their lives as members of Christ's body, the church. Some function like hands, like eyes, like feet and so on. Each has a place. Some members of the body may appear to have few, if any, gifts. Super-Christians would look down on them. As usual, Paul turns that logic upside down. " . . . the parts of the body which seem to be weaker are indispensable. . . . God has so adjusted the body, giving the greater honor to the inferior part, that there may be no discord in the body" (1 Cor. 12:22-25).

Putting that in modern terms Paul means that those Christians in our midst who "appear" (note how Paul qualifies his judgment) to be less gifted are to be most honored. There is a tendency among neo-Pentecostals to glorify those who "appear" to have the most gifts. Great rejoicing is heard when someone receives a spiritual gift, like tongues. According to Paul, such an emphasis is out of balance. We can certainly rejoice when one among us is gifted in one way or another for ministry in the body. We are called, however, to accord the highest honor to those who seem to be the weaker members of the body. The greatest honor does not belong to the one with the most impressive list of spiritual gifts. Greatest honor goes to those who appear weak among us. That way there is harmony in the body. That way no one has anything to boast of. "Let him who boasts, boast of the Lord" (1 Cor. 1:31).

With this material as background let us see how Paul understands and interprets spiritual gifts.

1. The first principle we learn from Paul is that *spiritual gifts are given to the community through individuals.* That is why Paul's lists of spiritual gifts include very ordinary matters. These gifts do not have the function of marking off those who are "truly spiritual" from those who are carnal or fleshly. Spiritual gifts are not signs of our super-Christianness. Spiritual gifts are given to a variety of the members of the Christian community in order that the whole body of Christ *on earth* might be strengthened. Gifts of the Spirit have a corporate rather than an

individual focus. Gifts of the Spirit are a call to service, not a sign of higher righteousness.

2. According to 1 Corinthians 13 the *greatest gift of the Spirit is love*. 1 Corinthians 13 is deliberately placed between chapters 12 and 14. It is the heart of the matter for Paul. "Love never ends; as for prophesies, they will pass away; as for tongues, they will cease; as for knowledge, it will pass away" (1 Cor. 13:8). For Paul the shape of love was determined by the shape of Christ and the shape of Christ was the shape of the cross. The cross is the sign that "God so loved the world that he gave his only Son" (John 3:16). God's love cost him his son. God's love gives itself away freely for all people. The God who is the Father of Jesus Christ gives his love away. That's what the cross means. It's the shape of a love that never stops giving.

The gifts of the Spirit (charismata) are to take the form of the cross. Christian love looks like the cross. It is a love that keeps on giving. Spiritual gifts should be measured by that very earthly criterion. They are means of giving to others. What has been given to us is to be passed on and on and on. We are edified in order that others may be mutually edified.

Anyone seeking to come to terms with the neo-Pentecostal movement must come to terms with Paul's letters to the Corinthians. Spiritual gifts belong to the community. Spiritual gifts are to take the shape of the cross (love). That is Paul's advice. If the church today follows that advice it will welcome all the *gifted ones* (charismatics) into its midst. If neo-Pentecostals take Paul seriously they will find their place within the body of Christ, giving their life and love for all in need. *This corporate or communal aspect of the gifts of the Spirit cannot be overemphasized.*

# 10

# Feathers Revisited

Involvement in the neo-Pentecostal movement began for me in Ethiopia more than a decade ago. My first reactions included surprise, excitement, joy, confusion, and an eagerness to share my experience. I shared my experience. I told my story. Many thought I had swallowed the Holy Spirit, "feathers and all."

It's time now to assess what all of this has meant for my life as a child of God. What difference has it made in my life? How have I changed? What has happened to me over these years? Many people ask me those exact questions. I have puzzled long and hard over an adequate answer.

The answers I have arrived at are, of course, intensely personal. As I share them with you it is important to understand a number of things. First, I am not saying that involvement in the gifts of Spirit will produce similar results in everyone. Second, I don't know what would have happened to me during these years if this neo-Pentecostal experience had not happened to me. Maybe many of the same things! I don't know. Third, we should acknowledge that each of us is probably the worst judge of what has really happened in our own spiritual life. God alone knows who we are in his sight. The Christian community that surrounds us may also see us more clearly than we see ourselves. Those who know me best could probably write this chapter much better than I can.

*I have learned to be surprised by the Spirit.* No one could have been more surprised than I was the night my tongue first broke loose in bursts of sound. I was dumbfounded. The Spirit swept me off my feet as he nearly swept my tongue out of my mouth. That was an *extraordinary* surprise. Strange as it may seem, however, that has led me to expect surprises of the Spirit in what might be called the *ordinary* workings of the Spirit.

You've detected a very strong emphasis in this book on the Word (the Bible and the shared word of believers) and the sacraments (baptism and the Lord's Supper). Those are the places we expect the Spirit to do his work. I had read about that in books. I learned it from the Small Catechism. Somehow all those words suddenly became alive for me.

The Spirit had to catch me off guard, it seems, to show me that he is constantly at work in my life and in the lives of others. The Spirit animates God's Word and makes it live. He really does. He calls people all the time. He grabs them up into his life and mission. He turns them on to newness of life in his name. It surprised me to realize how potent and dynamic the Spirit's work in the ongoing life of the church really is. I'm constantly surprised at what the Spirit accomplishes through the Word. I'm constantly surprised at what the Spirit does to people through the sacraments. The Spirit is full of surprises. He works them all the time. He works them wherever two or three are gathered in his name.

The Spirit surprises! I'm surprised at the gifts he pours out on his church. I've had to learn to have an open mind regarding gifts of the Spirit, healing and so on. But I'm most surprised at what the Spirit accomplishes in the on-going, everyday, seemingly normal work of the church. I think it's fantastic. The Spirit is fantastic. The gospel he empowers is fantastic. I'm constantly amazed and surprised at the way God's Spirit transforms and reshapes the lives of countless men and women through the "ordinary" means of Word and sacrament.

> O the depth of the riches and wisdom and knowledge of God! How unsearchable are his judgments and how inscrutable his ways! (Rom. 11:33).

*I have learned the meaning of the fellowship and com-munion of the Holy Spirit in ever new ways.* That should have been evident in Chapter 2 as I described the prayer fellowship I became a part of. That helped me to under-stand the meaning of the Christian church. The church is the fellowship of forgiven sinners. God accepts us into his fellowship *not because of* what we are but *in spite of* our weaknesses and shortcomings.

Christians are forgiven people. Forgiven people forgive. I had known well the meaning of God's forgiveness. It has been refreshing to experience the forgiveness of the com-munion of saints. It has been good to be able to go to the community of believers with my hurts and pains and problems. It's been good to be able to make public con-fession there of my shortcomings and still be accepted. I have been accepted when I felt so terribly unacceptable. I have been prayed for in prayers that expressed far better than I could the wounds of my being. That's community. That's communion. The communion of saints. Thank God for them. Thank God for the church. Thank God for one place on this earth where I don't have to *prove* my worth and acceptability. Thank God there are people who can love unlovable people like me.

This experience of community has led to community in another sense. For the past few years my family has lived communally with another family. Not surprisingly that family was part of our initial experiences in Ethiopia so many years ago. In the sense in which one feels *called* to something, we have certainly felt called to a communal life style.

Intense communal living teaches many lessons that might not otherwise be learned in a lifetime. I once heard the head of a Catholic monastery say that monastic, i.e., communal living, is like taking a bunch of rough rocks, putting them into a bag, and shaking them and bumping them against each other until they are smooth. The description fits. Just as the community *accepts* you as you are, it also *exposes* you for what you are. That's certainly been true for me. (I think the others would say the same thing.) I've learned things about myself I would have preferred not to know! I don't like what I've learned. It could lead to despair. I've been close to that. Or, it can lead to an ever deeper dependence and trust in the God of grace. I hadn't realized how much of myself his grace had to cover. Amazing grace!

I have also learned that the church could profit from more small group encounters between its members. No one enjoys a large and powerful worship service any more than

I do. Such services have been and will always be an integral part of our Christian life together. Our large gatherings, however, need to be balanced with more opportunities for small gatherings. The format can vary. (The church must learn to live with variety!) The small group can be a prayer group, an encounter group, a Bible study group, a rap group. All of these can exist in the same congregation. Any of them may serve as meaningful places of communication. Communication creates community. According to the Pentecost account in Acts 2:7-8, part of the task of the Holy Spirit is the task of making communication possible where it appeared to be impossible.

The Spirit can create new Pentecosts among us. He can enable us to communicate. The church as the communion of saints is a communicating body. Small groups may serve as the Spirit's workshop in enabling communication.

*I have learned to take prayer more seriously and more expectantly.* Prayer is dependence on God. In that sense our whole lives as Christians are lives of prayer. In the narrower sense prayer is the vocalization of that dependence. The language of prayer is the language of dependence. I think that is why it is sometimes hard for us, for me at least, to pray in a group. When I pray aloud in front of others I have to drop all of my masks and speak from my heart. I guess there are times I'm not sure I want others catching such deep glimpses of my being.

In recent years prayer has become more meaningful for me. To deny that would be to deny clear fact. I have prayed more. I have prayed more in groups and in my closet. I've seen many prayers answered in what appeared to be miraculous ways. I've become more serious about my prayer life. I've learned to pray expectantly. God does answer our prayers. He doesn't always answer them in the ways we would like but he hears and acts. When we put our lives in his hands he cares for us. Dependence (prayer!) on God is the heart of the matter for Christians.

*I have learned to quietly trust God with my todays and tomorrows.* When I was in college and seminary I constantly was wondering what my future would hold. I had so many plans. So many possibilities. (I had so many life-plans figured out that it would have taken five people to fulfill them all!) When I look back on those dreaming days I sometimes want to throw my head back and laugh at myself. I had plans. Big plans. None of them came true in the way I imagined they might. God kept surprising me with his plans, his call. He led me to places I had never dreamed of. What has happened in my life is not what I planned! I could never have planned or dreamed up the kind of life and excitement God has provided for me. I don't plan very much any more. God holds my tomorrow in his hand. I don't know what it is. I know it's better than any I could plan.

Much of this lesson has been learned through prayer and through interpretations and prophecy. God's promises have been clear. "I'll take care of you. I was before you. I come after you. I walk with you. Trust me." I've tried to. I've tried to entrust my life into God's hands. I don't always succeed. There's always that little voice inside of me that says I could figure out my life better than God can. I try not to listen to that voice. I've learned something of God's care and guidance. My future is a bright one. I have no idea what it will be like. But God is there. He'll probably surprise me again with his call to unknown (unknown to me) worlds of service. I'll await his call. God has taught me to be patient.

I could go on. I could cite what I see happening in the lives of others caught up in the neo-Pentecostal movement. The exhilarating sense of joy. The excitement about life with God. A new love and interest in the Bible. The sense that God speaks to and cares for each of us in a personal way.

I could cite more facts, more stories, more instances from my own life. Such a "feathers and all" testimony, however, may miss the point. The real point that emerges through all of this personal testimony should be a witness to the grace of God. I don't want you to put this book down remembering me and my experiences. I want you to put it down having heard again the "old, old story of Jesus and his love." It's a true story! Jesus is God's love for sinners . . . only for sinners. The Holy Spirit makes that love happen today for you and for me. That's Spirit Baptism! The Spirit wills to drown and dunk and immerse us daily in the love of God.

The Spirit works. I believe he has worked in me. I believe he has worked and continues to work in you. Everyday of our lives the Spirit wills to come to us with his life-creating work. He is at work when we daily renew our baptismal covenant. He is at work in God's Word as we read it, share it and hear it. He is at work in the bread and the wine of the Lord's Supper. We ought to expect him to work his transforming work on us in ever new and surprising ways. Don't box him in. Let him do for you what he wills. Let him do for you what he sees to be your need. Let him do for you what the community needs from you.

He may give you the gift of tongues. He can do that. He may give you the gift of healing. He may give you the gift of teaching or administration or concern for the outcast and down-trodden or any of an endless number of gifts. Accept what he gives you. Don't tell him what you need. Let him give to you as the sovereign Spirit. Be open to all the Spirit's gifts.

Openness. Expectancy. That's how we live out our lives under the Spirit's lordship. We don't possess the Spirit after all. The Spirit possesses us. Our prayers, therefore, are always addressed to the *coming* Spirit. Our daily prayer might well be the words of an ancient hymn:

> Come, Holy Ghost, our souls inspire
> And lighten with celestial fire;
> Thou the anointing Spirit art
> Who dost thy sevenfold gifts impart.
>
> Praise to thy eternal merit,
> Father, Son, and Holy Spirit. Amen.

Breathe on me, breath of God. Touch me with your Spirit. In your touch, from your breath, we have our life and our being.